D1309600

Okavango
Africa's Last Eden

Peter Johnson & Anthony Bannister
Text by Creina Bond

Okavango

Africa's Last Eden

Country Life Books

Contents.

To Claire and Maud-Anne

Distributed for Country Life Books by
The Hamlyn Publishing Group Limited
London · New York · Sydney · Toronto
Astronaut House, Feltham, Middlesex, England

This edition first published 1978

ISBN 0 600 36751 7

Foreword.

Where water spreads out over otherwise dry land it becomes of interest to all people and an almost irresistible attraction to engineers and developers. All of Africa's great swamps from the Nile Sudd to the Okavango have received attention from those who want to do something different with the land or water. Wetlands are usually highly productive ecosystems, and most tropical swamps are unusually productive. The productivity, however, is not expressed simply in some readily harvestable crop, but in a myriad of ways. The species of plants and animals that partake of and contribute to this productivity may defy any easy analysis. Primitive peoples have learned to adapt, to live in harmony with, and thrive on this complexity of life. The technicians of the modern world are less patient, less willing to understand diversity, to use what the natural world can of itself produce. Instead, where diversity occurs in rainforest or swampland we find efforts to simplify, to narrow the range, and force the system into directions determined by mankind. Thus swamps are drained, their waters channelled elsewhere, their life destroyed. Perhaps it did not matter when people were few and wild nature was in the ascendant. But it has happened too often in too many places. Now that wildness everywhere is threatened such losses are less tolerable.

In Botswana water is scarce and precious. Its presence determines how well people survive, its absence leaves large areas uninhabitable. Yet Botswana has one of the world's great wetlands where the abundance of water *limits* human occupancy. The contradiction brings temptation to change the pattern, to direct the water elsewhere. It is easy to measure short-term gains that could result from water transfer. It is much more difficult to quantify the long-term losses that would result from the impairment or destruction of one of the world's great wildlife habitats. One could reasonably ask that, for once, sufficient time be allowed for comprehension of the real values of the natural diversity of the Okavango, and for developing the means for maintaining a sustainable balance between natural requirements and human demands.

Unlike most African nations Botswana is still blessed with a richness of wildlife that will grow in value as time passes and the world changes. The original people of Botswana survived and lived well with only that wildlife to support them. It is an open question whether people could long survive the disappearance of wildlife. One hopes it will not be put to the test. So, let us consider the Okavango.

Raymond F. Dasmann
Chief Ecologist
International Union for the Conservation of Nature and Natural Resources, Switzerland

1 Watery fingers of the Okavango River meander indolently over the thirstlands of north-western Botswana to create a vast and verdant delta of tree-fringed islands and secret waterways.

2 'He who pushes his pole too deep stays with it' goes an old swamp saying. As children, the river people learn to pole their dugout canoes through the tangled expanses of water that are the highways of the Okavango Delta.

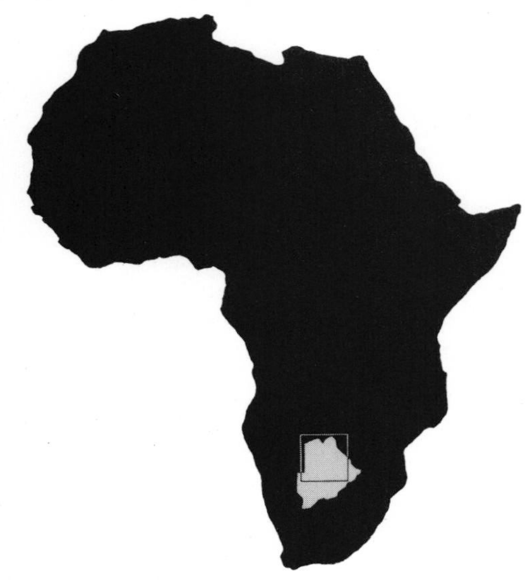

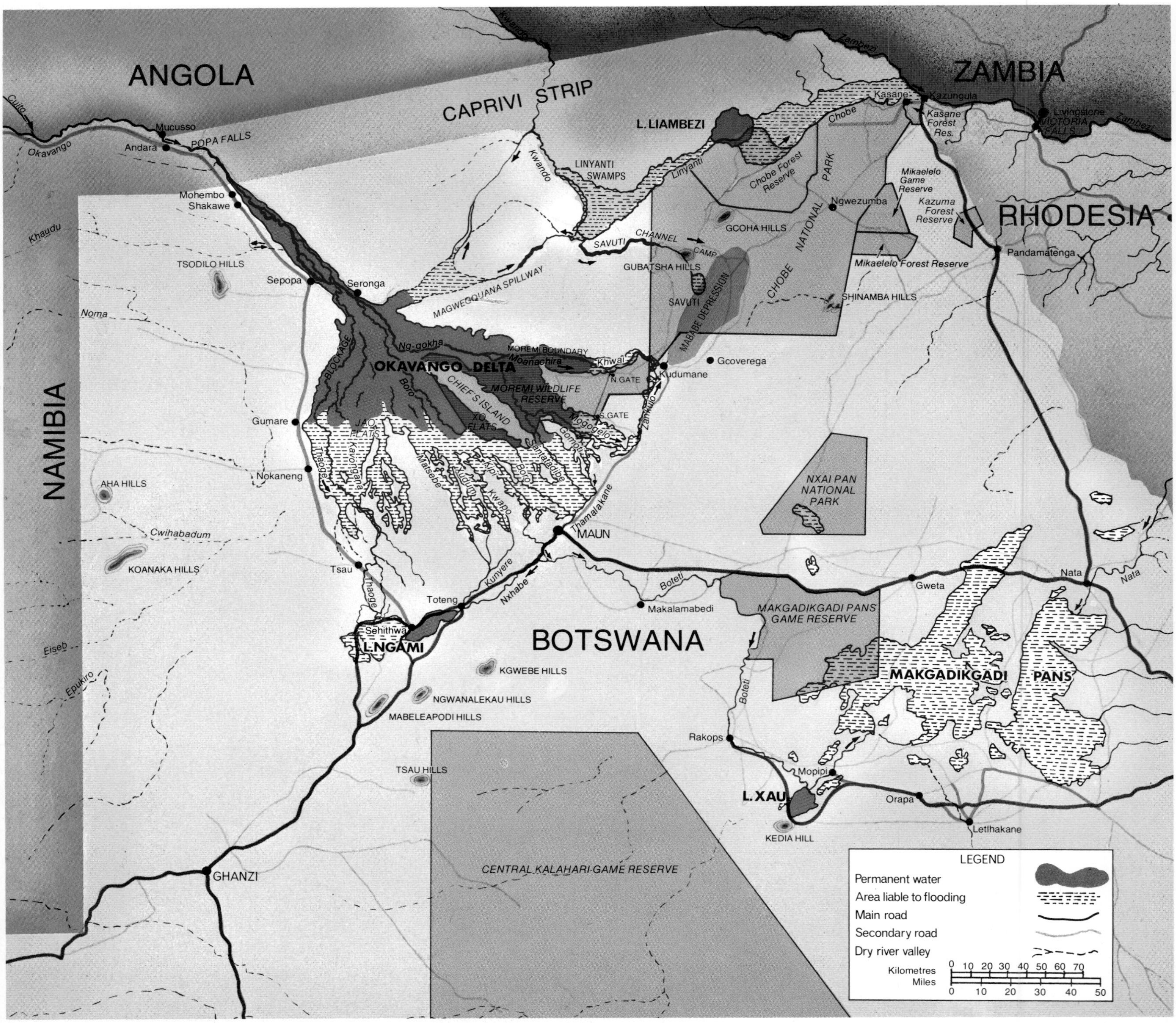

ANGOLA
ZAMBIA
CAPRIVI STRIP
NAMIBIA
RHODESIA
BOTSWANA
Cuito
Okavango
Mucusso
Andara
POPA FALLS
Kwando
Zambezi
L. LIAMBEZI
Kasane
Kazungula
Livingstone
VICTORIA FALLS
Kasane Forest Res.
Chobe
Linyanti
LINYANTI SWAMPS
Chobe Forest Reserve
CHOBE NATIONAL PARK
Mikaelelo Game Reserve
Kazuma Forest Reserve
Ngwezumba
GCOHA HILLS
SAVUTI CHANNEL
CAMP
GUBATSHA HILLS
SAVUTI
MABABE DEPRESSION
Pandamatenga
Mikaelelo Forest Reserve
SHINAMBA HILLS
Mohembo
Shakawe
Khaudu
TSODILO HILLS
Sepopa
Seronga
MAGWEGQUANA SPILLWAY
Noma
BLOCKAGE
Ng-gokha
MOREMI BOUNDARY
Moanachira
OKAVANGO DELTA
Khwai
Kudumane
Gcoverega
N GATE
Boro
CHIEF'S ISLAND
MOREMI WILDLIFE RESERVE
XO FLATS
JAO FLATS
S GATE
Mogogelo
Gomoti
Zankuio
Gumare
Nokaneng
Thaoge
Kavongana
Matsebe
Santantadibe
Kwapo
Thamalakane
NXAI PAN NATIONAL PARK
AHA HILLS
Cwihabadum
MAUN
KOANAKA HILLS
Tsau
Kunyere
Nxhabe
Boteti
Toteng
Sehithwa
L.NGAMI
Makalamabedi
MAKGADIKGADI PANS GAME RESERVE
Gweta
Nata
MAKGADIKGADI PANS
Eiseb
Epukiro
KGWEBE HILLS
NGWANALEKAU HILLS
MABELEAPODI HILLS
Rakops
Mopipi
TSAU HILLS
L. XAU
Orapa
Letlhakane
KEDIA HILL
GHANZI
CENTRAL KALAHARI GAME RESERVE
LEGEND
Permanent water
Area liable to flooding
Main road
Secondary road
Dry river valley
Kilometres 0 10 20 30 40 50 60 70
Miles 0 10 20 30 40 50

Introduction.

For an hour the landscape below had been unchanging. Only the altering patterns of bush and scrub told that the small plane was making progress. The earth stretched unendingly, blurred in the heat. 'There's nothing there,' complained the lady tourist. She shielded her eyes from the glare. 'What do people see in it?'

Only a nomad is at ease with space, unafraid that his tread has no echo. In Botswana footsteps fall on sands so deep they bury sound, muffle bedrock, flatten the sky. On and on go the heavy horizons, spread out over 2 500 000 square kilometres, the greatest mantle of sand in the world, the desert of the Kalahari.

Here is a thirstland with no certainties, and with few explanations. Stranded on its surface are the dusty bones of other landforms, relicts of prehistory. What happened to the ancient lakes that left their shorelines etched on sand? Why did the rivers retreat, abandoning their channels? Did the earth groan one day and topple its fossil rivers? Even now there are hidden thuds of turmoil.

'In the afternoon of the 25th, it being a very fine day, we were startled by a most unusual sound and a loud rumbling like subterranean thunder.' With these words pioneer hunter-trader James Chapman made the first report of an earthquake in Botswana in January 1854. 'It seemed approaching nearer and nearer and we saw everything visibly shake before our eyes. In an instant the whole town was in alarm, the women rushing out of their huts with clubs and hoes in their hands, holding them up at the sky and cursing God with the most awful imprecations. After an instant's cessation there was another shock, accompanied by a crash which was even louder than the first. Some of the women lost their footing as they stood rending the air with their demoniacal yells.'

Nearly 100 years later the sands were still unsteady with the grumble of earthquakes. With the force of exploding megaton bombs, 23 earthquakes shuddered underground in the 13 months from May 1952.

'This morning's tremor brought down the bulging stoep walls of the old Assistant District Commissioner's House,' notes an official report from Maun to the Public Works Department.

The Boro River that had been almost dry for 30 years began to flow again.

On average, three earthquakes a year still ripple below the sands and scientists in South Africa, France, America, pick up the tremors on their instruments and pinpoint the centre of the quakes. It lies beneath the waters of the Okavango.

David Livingstone, the missionary doctor, was among the first of the early explorers to reach this lost world. Tantalised by African stories of an inland lake far across the desert, he set off with some friends in 1849 to pull their wagons across the unknown Kalahari and discovered not only Ngami, but the outskirts of the Okavango. 'We came to a large stream,' he wrote. 'I enquired whence it came. "Oh, from a country full of rivers, so many that no one can tell their number – and full of trees" . . . We found the water to be so clear, cold and soft the higher we ascended that the idea of melting snow was suggested to our minds.'

The Okavango is born, not as snow, but as trickles of summer rain in the mountains of Angola. From the start it is a wayward child. Just 300 kilometres from Africa's Atlantic coastline the highland streams gather together and strike vainly across the vast face of the subcontinent in search of another

3 It is here among the blinding salt and crazed mud crust of the Makgadikgadi Pans that the waters of the great Okavango River seep to their final resting place in the Kalahari sands.

sea, the Indian Ocean some 3 000 kilometres to the east. When it reaches the plain it is a swift deep river which flows 1 000 kilometres before its torrent falters, a hesitant invader of the Kalahari desert. Then, sagging on sands 300 metres deep, disturbed and disordered by jolts in the earth's crust, the river spills into the braided channels, the swamps and lakes and lagoons of a 15 000 square kilometre wilderness. Where other rivers seek the ocean shores, the Okavango forms its delta on a sea of fitful sand.

The Okavango is a place of restlessness. The rivers are beautiful but deranged. Channels flow one way this year, another way the next. Seemingly perverse, the floods pour down in the dry season when no rain falls. They get narrower, not wider as they run their course. A few steadily climb up above the countryside as if to defy the laws of waterflow.

Yet these are the streams that feed the long, waving beds of papyrus, the hippo grass and waterlilies that tangle the edges of the waterways. They feed the crocodile and hippo, the buffalo and elephant, the secretive aquatic antelope cowering in the wet greenery, the noisy babbler in the reeds, and the fish eagle watching from the sky. This is Botswana's sea of land, land of water.

The maps are wary of admitting roads. On the flats and ridges of sand, the roads and tracks seem as aimless as the game paths. Those you find fan out, converge, separate again and sometimes disappear in a churn of dust. Across the sands there are no destinations, just the endless movements of the wild herds, their coming and going only as predictable as the summer storms. And there is restlessness, too, in the people who wander from village to cattle post, from upriver to downriver and back again.

Man has probably lived on the edge of the Okavango for at least 100 000 years. But the Okavango's modern history belongs to the newcomers, recent arrivals of less than 200 years ago. Until that time there were only a few scattered bands of baNoka, or River Bushmen, who roamed where they could along the Okavango's winding waterfronts. Then at different times, from different directions, came the baYei, the haMbukushu, the baTawana, baKalahari, the ovaHerero – many tribes sharing a diversity of skills to adapt to the rhythms of their unique environment.

The first of the new tribes were the baYei. With their coming in 1750 the Okavango found its real masters, for the baYei came from the swamp country of the Caprivi; they were people who knew the river as a friend. They like to boast: 'We are like the current of a mighty stream that cannot be stopped. We make our way through the thickest thickets.'

David Livingstone encountered the baYei on his journey to Lake Ngami and said of their legends: 'They have a tradition that their forefathers, in their first essays at war, made their bows of the Palma Christi, and when these broke they gave up fighting. They have never been known to use arms and have invariably submitted to the rule of every horde which has overrun the countries adjacent to the rivers on which they love to dwell.'

Livingstone liked 'the frank and manly bearing' of these men and instead of a wagon preferred a seat in one of their canoes. 'They always have fires in them and prefer sleeping in them to spending the night on shore. "On land you have lions," they say, "serpents, hyaenas and your enemies, but in your canoe behind a bank of reed nothing can harm you." '

Livingstone's brief journey to the Okavango country was to bring great changes to its peoples. For

4 Massed for safety, Cape Buffalo taste the cool morning air for scent of danger. Huge herds of game are drawn inexorably to the Okavango's promise of lush grasses and gentle waters.

him the unknown was incentive enough, but his companions were after other rewards. They had heard 'flaming accounts of the quantities of ivory to be found there . . . cattle pens made of elephant tusks of enormous size.'

A trader in his party, wrote Livingstone, 'was purchasing ivory at the rate of ten good large tusks for a musket worth thirteen shillings. The tusks were called bones and I myself saw eight instances in which the tusks had been left to rot with the other bones when the elephant fell. In less than two years after our discovery not a man of the baTawana could be found who was not keenly alive to the value of the article.'

Five years after Livingstone's visit, James Chapman was in Botswana to hunt and trade. 'Trading with the native is a most tedious and vexatious affair,' he complained. 'The palmy days of trade are gone.' Yet, despite his complaints, he purchased tusks for 'a blue and pink bead which was very much in demand', and loaded his wagon so full of ivory that the oxen could not pull it up the rises.

In a single year, 1867, it was estimated that the tusks of 12 000 elephant passed through the hands of the traders at Shoshong on the edge of the desert. A new interior had been opened.

With the ivory trade, Africans obtained muskets and went after big game. Soon rhino had been exterminated, buffalo driven north and elephant so depleted that only 2 000 remain in the Okavango Delta today.

The tusk trade may be long dead but you can still find black hunters armed with muzzle-loaders, the crumbling wooden stocks painstakingly repaired with waterbuck skin. Ammunition has been updated; hunters buy gunpowder from the trading store and hammer lead from car batteries or scrounge airstrips for the seals off petrol drums to make musket balls.

Fishermen who once knotted nets of hibiscus fibre now unravel the nylon cord in discarded car tyres – and the wise fisherman keeps a spare on hand.

Even the oxpecker has seen a change in lifestyle. When it comes to ticks, the birds would seem to say as they jostle for a perch on a friendly backbone, donkey or buffalo taste much the same.

Today there are more than 40 000 people living in and around the Delta and 70% of them earn no salary, own no cattle, but live off the land as they have always done. At the waterside women gather perfume from dried grass stems, or pluck waterlily bulbs for the evening stew. Then it seems that time will never catch up on this corner of Africa after all.

Impressions.

Anthony Bannister never got beyond one small pool on his first visit to the Okavango, and the pool confused him. He was standing waist-deep in waterlilies photographing insects when the reeds swished and a man in a dugout appeared. Where had he come from? 'Up north,' Tony was told. 'A long, long way through the reeds.' It had seemed an independent pool but now Tony began to wonder what lay beyond its margins, how his pool could be part of the Okavango system. He had to go back many times before he understood the complexities of the swamps, before he could make sense of the underlying simplicity of the Okavango's waters.

Peter Johnson discovered the Okavango from the air, yet even at a height the landscape is bewildering. A pilot unfamiliar with the Delta can be as lost as a man seeking landmarks on the ocean. An island might be a landmark – unless there are islands beyond count. A tree can be a landmark – unless there are forests of trees. And a river, too, is a landmark, but only while there are no horizons wound with twisted ribbons of water.

As for myself, I found the Okavango along a river that got narrower and narrower until it disappeared in a bed of high reeds. 'It is not the end,' said the boatman, so we lifted the grounded canoe and pushed it through the reeds and suddenly, a long way ahead, we emerged onto a wide blue lake of rushing water. We were in the Okavango Delta and the flood was coming in.

By different means, from many edges, we have entered the Okavango, alone or together over the years.

This is a story made up of those many journeyings. In the Okavango all journeys eventually are one.

The River.

When God created the haMbukushu, he let them down on a rope from heaven to the Tsodilo Hills. And there on the rocks, tradition has it, you will find the footprints of the first men and their animals.

Yet it is not the haMbukushu who marked these sheer rock faces that rise so abruptly 400 metres above the sands, these hills that brood in their isolation over the pervading flatness of northern Botswana. A thousand years ago unknown artists covered the hills with friezes that are faded now, and torn, and as mysterious to the Bushmen who still hunt there as to the solitary visitors who sometimes scramble among the cliffs. Nobody has yet explored all Tsodilo's caves and overhangs, or climbed all the precipices that pile one upon another, their hot ledges watched over by basking snakes. The rock faces glow with the ochres and greens and golds of vivid lichens which may be more enduring than the paintings, for Tsodilo's great slabs are so friable that a thumb can rub the rock away.

The paintings are a riddle. There are more than 1 000 of them, most on exposed faces, some so high above the ground that they cannot be seen. Who did these paintings? And why did the artists never once draw the hippo or crocodile of the Okavango's waters less than 50 kilometres to the east?

When the haMbukushu dropped from heaven, they soon turned their steps away from Tsodilo, out across the desert to the waiting river with its clear swift currents glinting in the sun.

While the first haMbukushu may have dropped from heaven, others came fleeing along the river about 100 years ago, refugees from war and slavery. And they only beached their small canoes when they seemed too remote, too far from anywhere to be governed or ordered or sold. There they built the first walls of woven reed, clusters of huts with palisades that curled along the bank. The haMbukushu brought iron with them for spears and hoes, and they carried seed from the gardens they had left behind. Sorghum, millet, melons, gourds, pumpkins, beans – soon the new plants were rooting on land cleared along the river and after the harvest, drums thudded a thanksgiving for the crop.

But they were not the first people on the river: the baNoka or River Bushmen had been there long before, hunting in the forests along the water. The tribes met in friendliness and they bartered fish and meat for corn and iron. Particularly for iron. The Okavango country had no metals. On long river trips back to their old homeland the haMbukushu punted to fetch the iron, and so became the middlemen for long-distance trade between the Zambezi and the Delta. On the banks of the Okavango their reed-woven settlements prospered and grew.

And this is where our Okavango journey begins, at Shakawe, capital of the north, trading centre for all of upper Ngamiland, Botswana's northern district. Today there are the people of many tribes and hundreds of huts sit above the river in an untidy scramble of mud walls and sinuous paths. It is a place where they tell the time by the sun's elevation, where women with baskets scoop fish from the river, where men sign up for stints on the mines.

Shakawe is a capital which has planted its walls carelessly among the spires of an older and more serious society – the termites or white ants. The people may be languid with the heat and the beer and the song of the river, but the termites never cease their industry.

'I can be sure I'm in Africa when I drop my trousers on the floor at night – and find the termites have eaten holes in them by morning,' a friend once said. Shakawe certainly offers that assurance. But while the termites consume every remnant of rag and grass and wood and paper, the people soon reciprocate by consuming the termites.

'Those that have eaten the locust prefer the white ant,' said nineteenth-century explorer James Chapman, extolling the virtues of this acquired taste. 'Hunger will create an appetite for strange viands and it was after suffering three days of starvation that driven by necessity, I learnt to relish the insects.' On warm summer evenings lamps bob among Shakawe's mud spires as the town's citizens collect their favourite cocktail snack. Impelled by summer's thunderstorms, the termites emerge in their thousands upon thousands, a steady procession of kings and queens-to-be. The insects have never seen the light, they have never flown before, but they flutter up on gossamer wings to find a destiny – and a gobbling crowd makes sure that they don't have to seek far. Children fill their pails and the sky wheels and dives with hunting birds grabbing a meal from the royal exodus. Even kites clumsily stuff their beaks mid-air using talons designed for other prey. In the Okavango there are termite spires all along the way.

There have been changes at Shakawe in a hundred years but the Okavango itself is little changed. It remains an open river 100 metres across on a floodplain many times as wide. The river's call has made for a restless people, always coming and going, following the tug of a morning breeze, chasing the clouds in their small canoes.

Shakawe lies on the border of three countries – Botswana, Namibia and Angola – but a river knows no frontiers and river people are the same. They glide from country to country with neither passport nor visa. They reason: 'Isn't it one riverbank all the way?'

There are fewer hippo than there used to be in the Okavango, but they still lord it in the main channels, and even at Shakawe insist on their right of way. The people don't argue. A distant grunt is enough to send a dugout shooting for the bank, spilling frightened passengers. Angry yells from people stranded on the far bank leave the ferryman unmoved.

'They're telling that man he bloody fool,' a small boy explains. But even if there's not another grunt for hours the bloody fool takes no chances and his mokoro stays moored without a fare.

Mekoro, or dugout canoes, are the taxis of the Okavango. You can hire one for $6 a day or even buy one as Anthony Bannister and Peter Johnson discovered when they followed a trail of wood chips while looking for a mokoro under construction in a northern Okavango village.

'Now what a pity,' they were told. 'Mbini has a new one but he's just taken it downriver. And Mr Sese had one but he's gone to plough.'

But there was one master craftsman neither visiting nor ploughing, Kay Dumile. Yes, he could make the white man a mokoro. The standing price was two to four cattle for a four-seater, and the customer, of course, must choose his own tree.

Once the northern villages were surrounded by hardwood forest but the trees are so scattered now that even the tough green skins of monkey oranges are carved with the marks of children making an early claim to their share of the crop. And so the boat-builder led them on a tour among giant trees he had already marked as his own. It takes 100, 200, 500 years to grow a tree big enough for a mokoro – with a river life guaranteed for only five. However, when the leaks get so bad that the boat must be retired from the water, it converts very neatly into sledge, trailer or ambulance. The dusty mekoro lined up on the sand at Shakawe's weekly clinic show that dugouts have a useful future as land-based, ox-drawn vehicles long after their river days are done.

'*Mokutshumo* – it's the best wood for boats,' Kay advised. And the final choice was *mokutshumo*, or wild ebony. They chose an ancient tree with three trunks, each about 25 metres high: one trunk for the mokoro, one for shade, and one for the countryside and the glossy starlings and go-away birds, the green pigeons and parrots and hornbills that feed on the *mokutshumo's* sweet golden fruit.

Kay had two helpers, his colleague, Mateus, and his son Dinyando, and for two and a half weeks their axes shaped a prow in the living trunk. Only then did the tree fall, sighing in its branches, and a month later the dugout was ready, a rose-coloured, wide-bellied boat: 'Good for a white man; he won't fall out,' agreed the locals at the launching.

A mokoro soon cuts a white man down to size. You have to try one, swirling, revolving, wavering helplessly, before you can appreciate the skill needed to steer a banana, before you can learn an immutable law of the river: 'He who pushes his pole too deep, stays with it.' And first attempts with a keel-less, rudderless, hollowed-out tree trunk are recommended well away from the town and its cheering, cackling spectators.

'Hau. Hau. Hau.'

'Hau. Hau. Hau.'

The riverbank audience slaps its knees and roars with delight. 'Look at them drunk at this time of day!'

Shakawe's small fleets of mekoro lie out of sight of the village on sandy bays below the riverbank. Once a man could moor his mokoro and his boat was safe because he knew his neighbours. Today the wise captain has a chain and padlock to secure his vessel from strangers.

Travelling by dugout means a paddle for deep water, a pole for the shallows, a baling tin and a wet bottom; old or new, all mekoro have oozes. And the less you carry the better you go. The river may have many freedoms, but they belong to the man who carries his possessions with a shrug.

For the river people a mokoro is the only way to penetrate the Okavango, yet it seems a flimsy craft for a 650 kilometre journey.

From Shakawe the Okavango first runs 100 kilometres through the desert, sparkling on its bed of Kalahari sand. Below our mokoro the current whirls, picking up sand and cartwheeling it along the bottom. The grains spiral to the surface in a column of water, only to tango down the stream a few metres before falling back again. Every year two million tonnes of tiny grains bounce and roll in the rush of water, and where they settle at last they push the river bed higher and higher. But there is no way of sensing this when you are adrift on eddies of water and sky.

This always seems the longest part of an Okavango journey, hour after hour without variety. Water and sky. Water and papyrus. Round bend after bend we drift to more river and more sunlight and more papyrus. The mokoro rests so low in the water that the view is dominated by horizontal boundaries. We can never see far ahead and the same view repeats itself, hour merging into hour, water merging into sky, one long slow loop following another until we forget there is a world outside this waterway.

Yet the river does not look the same to the people of the Okavango; each section has a name of its own. *Bonga,* the Bushmen called it, *Xhi*, *Bakarakwe*, *Xangtsaudi*, *Kwadau*, *Wonga*, *Xwega*, *Qaoga* and *Xunxu* . . . the river had no single name.

We are not alone on the water. Skimmers glide from the sandbanks, splashing their feathers to cool their eggs back on the nest. Kingfishers bounce gently on swaying stalks to inspect the river, and bedraggled cormorants and darters dry their wings in the sun. There is other traffic on this part of the Okavango. With the twist and twirl of an expert oar a young boy shoots past, his mokoro piled high with reeds for sale in nearby villages. A family of six, packed among nets and spears and boxes, backpaddles for a greeting. The river is a friendly place. How are the people upcountry? Have there been rains? At home the birds have taken the corn crop . . .

There is no hurry to move on. A day is a tune of lap and splash and the bubbling sound of the coppery-tailed coucal.

Twelve hours beyond Shakawe we are still on what is called the 'panhandle', that part of the river which broadens out over a bed of desert sand, but not yet at the threshold of the sprawling Delta. On either side small villages still cluster out of sight yet not out of hearing and drums beat in the falling dusk.

A sandbank is the river traveller's resting-place for the night. Bellfrogs tinkle like windchimes and a thousand fireflies wink on the water. That distant splash could be a sitatunga leaving its island hideaway. Sometimes a fisherman will catch this strange antelope in his nets, but otherwise it is seldom seen – except from the air. Splayed hooves and a shaggy coat fit it for its life in the papyrus and if you do catch sight of one it bounds away, splashing and crashing through the reeds. Then, too suddenly, there is silence and a ripple. The sitatunga is a strong swimmer and when it is in hiding it can submerge itself underwater in a hole in the reed mat with just its beaky nose above the surface. There is no other large mammal confined to the permanent swamp, but the sitatunga is so seldom seen and so secretive that little is known of its niche in the Okavango.

Night is the time to look for crocodiles, for in bright lamplight their hot eyes glow at the river's edge. They are survivors of a lost world, and here in the darkness of the Okavango night one feels an awkwardness about one's own ancestry. What is 2 000 000 years to a reptile that glided at the feet of dinosaurs and pterodactyls? The crocodile outlived prehistory and its red night eyes tell of 50 million years of underwater silences and a scaly wisdom grown among waterlilies.

Some tribesmen revere this reptile, the haMbukushu catch it for the cooking pot – others leave it alone with a live-and-let-live. And until a fashion in handbags and shoes brought rifles in search of its soft underbelly skin the crocodile was found all over the Okavango. Bobby Wilmot, most famous of the crocodile hunters, killed thousands before he himself died in the swamps a few years ago of a black mamba bite. Commercial hunters have killed between 12 000 and 25 000 in the last 20 years. But when, in 1973, a private company obtained a concession to hunt 500 crocodiles in the Okavango panhandle, restrictions were such that by the second season it had to give up, unable to fill its quota. Lines of baby crocodiles still bob nose to nose beside the reeds but it is rare to see a big one. The papyrus has covered their retreat and for the moment the crocodiles can brood their nests in peace.

An Okavango dawn begins with dew showered from a million starry webs; first mokoro on the water snaps the threads of a night's endeavour and we glide with the wings of heron and egret and openbill stork dispersing for the day.

For a thousand years papyrus and river have struggled for the open currents. Here on the flat sands of the Kalahari where the water loses impetus, the papyrus moves in to conquer the flow, to turn river into swamp. Only in the deep waters of the northern swamp is that jungle of stem that sways and breaks and sinks, papyrus – the lawless green ruler of the Okavango's no-man's-land.

Men have tried to fight papyrus, hacking at its dense growth, but where a hundred plants fall a hundred more will rise again. Every month of the year explosions of fire roar across the water, the green adversary popping and spluttering in the flames. Sometimes a charred crocodile is left to float on a blackened grave. But the papyrus is already stirring among the ashes. Papyrus takes a long time to die.

Two or three days beyond Shakawe there is no doubt that the papyrus walls are squeezing the river into a narrower, slower channel. Here and there it still opens out to meet a tiny village on a sandy peninsula but there are fewer people on the water now. There is just the dazzle of heat on water, the quiet of the river's ripples, the swish of a bird at the water's edge. Here the papyrus asserts itself in a green revelry that tugs at the hesitant river, pulling it into loops, pushing it into backwaters, twisting and teasing across a wilderness 100 kilometres wide.

Man has never lived deep in the Okavango. He has always been a passerby, dreaming less of a home on the water than of a highway that could link him with distant places. This longing must have been strong even in the baNoka or River Bushmen, the first swamp people, for they had to follow the river on foot. They made rafts so that they could float on to pools to fish, but these frail heaps of reeds were never made for voyaging.

Our first peep into a sleepy backwater makes us realise, as others who have gone before, that the Okavango has many obstacles to communication. Swamp figs strangle the open water with spongy bogs that reverberate when you jump upon them. Hundreds of nesting heron and ibis and marabou squawk and jabber in the trees. The figs are inhabitants of old channels where the papyrus has ceded some territory.

The river flows on, back in the papyrus. Now and again a high-crowned palm tree leans against the sky. The first island appears, unapproachable, ringed with reed. We sense that we are losing our river, but deep in the papyrus we can see nothing of its slow dissolve; the deep clear water of a river that is now just 13 metres wide.

And, about 250 kilometres from Shakawe, we come to a sudden stop. The water flows on but we cannot float with it for ahead of us stretches the solid papyrus wall of the Nggoka blockage. And as we stare, disbelieving, at the vanished river, the plants laugh and leap and wave their fists, for we are not the first to be trapped at the Nggoka dead-end.

'All thoroughly exhausted,' wrote Mr V. Ellenberger in his logbook when he was halted by the blockage 46 years ago. 'Have no alternative but to spend the night in the boats. Mosquitoes bad. 10.15 p.m. Eclipse of the moon.'

Ellenberger, then Assistant Resident Magistrate for Ngamiland, had been sent on a five-week trip through the Okavango to explore a route for motor-boats. The magistrate hoped to cut through the papyrus by moonlight but the eclipse effectively stopped work and it was two days before he broke out of the jeering stalks. But he *did* eventually get through the blockage, which would be impossible today for the papyrus plug has grown 15 kilometres and it is too thick upstream and too dry in the middle. The Nggoka is a blind alley and when you get there, you and your mokoro have bumped into history.

The modern history of the Okavango began about 200 years ago when Hankuzi, a great hippo hunter, left his home in what is now the Caprivi on a hunt from which he would never return. Hankuzi had friends with him, fellow baYei, and they let their mekoro lead them from river to lagoon, through stream and marsh and channel and lake. Wherever there was water they could travel. Wherever there was hippo they would go. And as there was no end to the water, there was no end to their drifting, and weeks and then months rippled behind them, and dropped forgotten. So Hankuzi found the Okavango and it was not long before other baYei were punting and paddling their way to its islands and rivers, bringing with them skills that would open up the Delta, first with their dugouts and later with a new kind of raft.

'The most significant technological breakthrough in the Okavango was the introduction of the canoe and the papyrus raft,' claims Dr T. Tlou, the Botswana historian. The swamps were no longer a barrier to communication; people could move from the north, south all the way to Lake Ngami. And papyrus helped to show the way.

'Use of the new kind of raft was spread to all the swamps by the baYei and it is their invention,' says Dr Tlou. 'It is made by piling papyrus stems criss-cross around a central peg to which a rope is tied. Rafts are driven by the river current and so can only drift downstream. A typical raft could carry not only people, but belongings, food and boats. To stop, the raft was tied to a tree for as long as the group wanted to rest.'

And at the end of the trip?

The rafts were abandoned – it being very difficult to do anything else – and wedged in narrow river courses, the rafts took root and began to grow.

All the manipulations of the Delta have been designed to increase the flow of water one way or another, and Ellenberger's 56-page report was to result in the start of schemes that would include every sort of remedy from modern dredgers to papyrus hacks, injecting swamp figs with sulphuric acid, and making dams with holes in them.

Officialdom began with an assault on the Nggoka blockage. In 1932 Martinus Drotsky was employed to open it up. He had been born close to the Okavango and he knew there was only one way to live comfortably afloat deep in the papyrus – pitch camp on a papyrus raft. So he had 26 rafts made, and he and his labourers floated with the river down to the channel where they had to work. Drotsky lived in a tent on one raft – his men built huts on the others. Yet Drotsky had no illusions about the danger of rafts to the Okavango waters. In one spot he recovered 35 intact rafts that had been abandoned and he and his 100 workers obtained sufficient fuel from them to keep their campfires burning for six weeks.

However the work had not gone very far when some of the workers began to feel feverish. Soon men were collapsing, ill and dying in an influenza epidemic. Papyrus seemed unimportant.

Propping up the early schemes was the gusto of Colonel Charles Rey, Resident Commissioner, of itchy feet, iron will and strong prejudices. He roamed the territory in 'Topsy', his Armstrong-Siddeley Coupé, with Marzipan his driver, and not even the depression of the 1930s could shake him from his course once he had decided on the need for an Ngamiland waterway. There might be funds for nothing else, but there would be funds to clear the Okavango. What is more, Rey knew just the man for the job; Charles Naus, a traveller and hunter, a gentleman amateur who hadn't been at work long before he discovered what he believed would be the answer for the Okavango. He would build dams across several rivers to dry out their lower courses and burn away the plants. But when one of the dams was nearly finished Naus was impressed by the current sweeping through the small gap which remained to be closed. He thereupon abandoned his idea of drying up the riverbed and he formed instead the curious theory that dams with gaps in them somehow increased the flow!

Even Colonel Rey was sceptical, but his first look at a Naus dam convinced him. The rush of water through the hole spoke of a miracle. The Government Engineer advised against it, but the Government forked out funds for another five dams with holes. However, the problem was not, of course, solved. When Naus left, Martinus Drotsky came back and returned to orthodoxy, attacking the papyrus. For two years his men worked waist-deep in water, armed only with cane knives and sudd saws, until they pushed back the papyrus a record 100 kilometres in the Thaoge channel that reached for Lake Ngami further south. It was epic work and although the advance reclaimed only 1% of the swamp, nobody would manage as well again – not even W. G. Brind, the Government Engineer, with his marvellous merry-go-round.

Brind believed that hand-to-hand combat with the papyrus was effective only in shallow water. Once you reached deep water you needed something better, and so he designed a 45-ton rotary papyrus-cutting machine. The parts were made in South Africa and carted across the desert in lorries to be assembled at the site. But when the machine was winched into the swamps there were teething troubles. Surrounded by the papyrus it was supposed to defeat, the machine floated unused and unserviceable for years, and in 1957 was finally dismantled.

But even before Brind designed his machine something occurred which probably had more effect on the Okavango than all man's efforts. There was a severe earth tremor. Brind was upriver in the Okavango when it happened; for 45 seconds the earth trembled, paused, then shook again. On the next two days there were further tremors, that of the 13th being followed by intermittent rumbling for over ten minutes.

The Boro, described at the time as a 'trivial and wasteful river', broke open its old channel and began to flow strongly again. There is no certain way of finding out exactly what the earthquakes may have done to change the rivers, but they did nothing to diminish the papyrus.

The Delta.

For 250 kilometres we have run with the current, travellers on the mainstream of a great river. At the Nggoka blockage the mainstream dies but the river flows on through the swamp to give birth to other rivers beyond.

There are passages through the papyrus, although only the river people know the labyrinths. Grasping at plants overhead they haul their mekoro into the gloom of the watery jungles, navigating the papyrus fastnesses, slithering, splashing, pushing through the swamps to find the brightness of a lake of waterlilies.

And this is another world – a world of islands and forests and silver rivers where the wild pang of the fish eagle falls from the sky and time is lost in a thousand meanders.

Charles John Andersson was on a hunting expedition in 1853 when he became the first white man to break through the 'dreary and monotonous marshes' to fall under the spell of the Okavango.

'On every side, as far as the eye could reach, lay stretched a sea of freshwater,' he said, 'in many places concealed from sight by a covering of reeds and rushes of every shade and hue; whilst numerous islands spread out over the surface and, adorned with rich vegetation, gave to the whole an indescribably beautiful appearance.

'I could have spent days under the shade of some of the ornamental trees, resounding at times with the wild notes of birds, whilst in the distance might be seen herds of the finest antelope tribe. Rhinoceroses, hippopotomi, buffaloes, sassabys, hartebeests, pallahs, reedbucks, leches, etc. were constantly seen . . .'

That was the Okavango of long ago, and time has brought change. The papyrus has shifted. Some dryland of Andersson's day has since become swamp, and what was swamp is now dry. Old rivers have died, new streams have been born, while the earth buckled and tilted, shifting the loose sands, altering the flow. But beyond the deep waters of the papyrus, beyond the swift, deep territory of the haMbukushu, there still lies the world which enchanted Andersson 125 years ago.

Here the water has no single course. It spreads out to merge and flow and drift and linger. Channel joins channel, only to separate as little streams that slip into lagoons and backwaters and wind and wander and at last find currents that will carry them away.

The crystal clear water tugs at underwater gardens, trailing plants with many-coloured stems. Red and gold and pale green . . . some plants never break the surface, some drift with dangling roots, undulating in the stream.

Far behind now lie the unvarying days of river and papyrus. Each bend of the day has a new perspective, each bend of the day has a new surprise, for in the inner Delta of the Okavango nothing is ever quite what it seems to be. Big rivers forget they have a destination, lost in steamy tangles of hippo grass and reed. Dry land lies beyond the reeds; or a new river begins to flow; sometimes there is the unexpected sunshine of boggy water-meadows where startled pygmy ducks dart beneath the lily pads.

However the inner Delta is not uninhabited. It is the lovely shallow-watered kingdom of the baYei, the masters of the swamps. Among these lakes and lagoons, rivers and pools lies the homeland which Hankuzi, the great hippo hunter, discovered for his people more than 200 years ago.

The baYei know the Okavango's loneliness and are not afraid of it. They are solitary travellers along its waterways; river gypsies with small camps where bundles of fish dry in the sun. But in the island country of the Okavango you can travel far and see nobody at all.

We knew nothing of island country of the Okavango when we came upon it one winter afternoon, punting through a sea of waterlilies as it was getting dark. The islands rose from the water all around us, nameless and unknown. Later there was to be a new island every night but that evening we floated irresolute, unpractised at choosing a realm for the night. And later we lay awake on our beds of dry grass listening to the palm fronds jostle and crackle and rattle and sigh.

But it does not take long to become an islander, to know the soft plop, plop, plop of magenta flowers raining down at dawn as baboons in the sausage tree above breakfast on nectar. Mists hang around the islands on winter mornings, damp white swirls that muffle the river flowing just beyond our fire. We make coffee, shivering, and pile dry wood on the flames, waiting for the mists to lift and the sun to warm the water. Only then do we explore the island we discovered in darkness. Sometimes we have one to ourselves, sometimes we are disturbed by other island dwellers; a covey of francolin, a flag-tailed warthog marching past to scuffle and snuffle down the bank.

Some islands are no more than a mound with a lonely palm, threaded between two streams. Some islands are ringed by forests of wild ebony, garcinias, rain trees, leadwood, tree gardenias, fat-podded sausage trees and yellow-armed figs, and the skeletons of ancients whose cracked heads are festooned with creepers and pitted with hives and nests.

Chief's Island is 1 000 square kilometres of wild country, a great expanse of dryland savanna and shallow little pans with brown water and bright green verges. Kudu keep to the thickets but on the open lawns close to water zebra and wildebeest graze warily, alert for lion in the long grass. Often you walk all day and see nothing but a frisky tail depart through the bush, but there are seasons when hundreds of animals gather at the waterline. Chief's Island has recently become a game reserve, a specially protected part of the Okavango. It is a territory so large that you would have to live there many months to get to know it well. Yet it is only a part of an even larger wildlife reserve, Moremi, set aside by the baTawana 15 years ago to protect the diminishing wildlife of their tribal lands. Moremi has tracks but no buildings so its tourists sleep beneath the stars and bath with hippo. This is a beautiful and unforgettable outskirt of the Okavango, but beyond the sedges of its shallow lagoons still more islands beckon on the water.

There are big islands and there are small islands, but nowhere among the gleaming water meadow is there one without a golden termite spire. Lie close to the heart of an island, and deep underground you may sense the faint whisperings and knockings. Then you know the island-makers are at work mixing mud to build eternity.

An island begins with one rain-wet particle moved in darkness by two lonely termites – a king and a queen beginning a new dynasty after their brief nuptial flight. Soon grain will follow grain, licked and rolled and excavated as passageways, shaped into galleries, engineered into arches and domes of perfect proportions by the growing throng of royal progeny. With the rainy season, each spire erodes a little to broaden its base and all the while the termites are busy repairing, rebuilding, pulling their citadel above the radiance of the water.

Then plants take root in the rich soil of the mound, and the first young tree claims a perch. Around the buttress lechwe make a look-out, or lion squat upon the spires, seeking elevation.

If an outsider smashes the mud walls the termites clear the dead, patch the debris and build again. Even if the queen dies of age or accident the colony lives on. Another sovereign is created, and another, and so the spires mark a society that could live forever.

The Delta

Nights in the island country of the Okavango are full of interruptions. Once Anthony Bannister was woken by an inexplicable sloof, sloof, sloof. He ran to the riverbank and there, by the light of his torch, he saw the strange pink eyes and waving whiskers of a thousand barbel moving through the water along the bank. Tails slapping, bodies rasping, mouths opening and closing, they moved on into the night in a queer spawning dance.

Strange sounds and stranger silences belong to the Okavango. Even the flood comes quietly.

The Okavango's flood marks the Delta's two seasons: one wet and one dry. Far north in Angola the flood begins, but it is six months before the first small ripple reaches Shakawe, followed by a swell that lingers and laps the bank until there is a new river, three metres deeper and 300 metres wide. But why is there this new river? Why does the water not soak down through the darkness of the Kalahari sand? The answer lies in the mysterious sea of fossil waters that saturates the sand below the Okavango. We know nothing of these fossil waters, where they come from, why they are there or even how old they are, except that they belong to prehistoric times. When the flood comes in it rides afloat last summer's storms, subdued by the still deeper waters of the hidden sea.

Even at its peak the flood is tranquil. One minute the ponds are still, then the lily leaves tremble to the silent inrush of currents.

For weeks the people have been waiting. 'Where is the flood?' the question buzzes up and down the villages of the Okavango. 'Where's the flood today?'

In dusty courtyards the news is passed around: 'It's got as far as Xunxu. That means next week the flood will be near . . .'

'It's on its way,' gossip the women over the supper pots. 'They say the flood is on the way.'

The men are restless as they pass the beer.

Winter dusts have bleached and withered the desert grasses and mud is cracking in the desert's drying pans when the flood brings its wash of wetness and greenery.

All summer, wildebeest and zebra have wandered in the dry country nibbling the desert's brief grasses, drinking at the little pans. But when the flood comes in 12 000 animals gather along the waterline of the Okavango. A thousand wildebeest canter in to water and a thousand zebra kick their heels and turn into the wind. Even 100 kilometres to the north buffalo lift their heads and sniff the breeze and thunder in on the scent of the flood. About 20 000 buffalo are to be found in the Delta for most of the year, herds of 70 to 200 spending the wet season among the rainwater pans of the sandveld, roaming in the Delta's mosaic of islands when it is dry elsewhere.

With seep and trickle and ooze the flood pushes the Okavango into new territory, doubling its size. Yesterday there was dust. Today lechwe leap in bounding cascades of watery sparks. Every year the flood shifts direction, one year flowing down a hippo track to fill an empty lagoon, leaving last year's inlet high and dry.

A plain that has been parched for 20 years is drenched once more, and waterfowl settle among its drowning trees. Where there was a chain of pools, now there is a cool, clear river that carries us to the margins of the sandy plains where giraffe lollop slowly over bronzed leaves of fallen mopane and elephant rattle nutty pods from tall acacias, where the smoke of hunters' fires comes drifting through the trees.

When the flood draws the scattered herds in from the desert, the hunters follow too, ready for a harvest that will mean food and clothing and items for barter. The hunters camp never far from water, the trees nearby festooned with long lines sagging under the burden of meat hung up to dry.

Every year 8 000 animals are killed in the Delta by 1 300 tribal and 200 recreational hunters. Most of the tribesmen are still after traditional prey – impala, buffalo, bushbuck, wildebeest, warthog, lechwe and tsessebe. The meat is salted and dried in the sun to be eaten later on. Hides are tanned at home and made up as trousers, caps, rugs, riems, sandals and even grainbags. And what the people do not use themselves they barter at the trading store for mealie-meal or sugar or tobacco.

But commercial hunting is increasing. Some black hunters now stalk lion, leopard or elephant for the cash reward. Others sell skins and meat and use the income to buy cattle. But the men hungry for cattle are not the traditional peoples of the Okavango and most of the livestock is owned by a few wealthy families. Only one baYei family in five owns any cattle at all and for these swamp people the Okavango continues to supply the resources they really need.

Some hunters reach the flood by following sandy paths on foot. Others pull their mekoro into the river, punting over waterlogged plains, and the liquid melodies of their *kalimbas* – their thumb pianos – travel with the boats. At floodtime there are many boats along the Okavango's waterways.

'Dumela,' men call out as they push their poles into the clean white sand. *'Dumela,'* the greeting is returned as they slip out of sight.

Not all the passing people are after meat. Some are honeyhunters and they are on the water every month of the year. Up and down the rivers they move, whistling to that little drab brown bird, the honeyguide. When they hear an answering call from the bush, man and bird track the bees together, whistle answering whistle as the bird shows the way to dripping combs in the cracks and holes of tall *mokutshumo* trees. And the honeyhunter is careful to reward the bird with part of the comb, for should he fail to do so, the next time the bird could lead him to a mamba – or so the story goes. There have always been hive-tappers along the waterways, gathering wild black honey to trade in villages far beyond the water.

In the 1930s rumour spread among the people of the reed-walled towns; honey ripened in the darkness of island forests, they said, was honey that could kill. *Kotsela* – the drowsy sickness. *Kotsela* came from honey. The whispers flickered and grew until the honey hunters were waved away. Nobody would eat the Okavango honey.

And the people were not entirely wrong in their fear. In Tanzania where about 500 people catch the sickness every year, a third get it while they are out on expeditions to gather wild honey. In Botswana *kotsela* belongs to the Okavango islands, to the shady places where the honey hunters spend their days searching among the trees. But *kotsela* comes not from honey, but from the tsetse, a biting fly that swarms the Delta's shade.

The tsetse is a bloodsucker that claims dominion over the Okavango, advancing its territory steadily in a 60-year war; villagers have retreated, fields have been deserted, grazing lands abandoned and left to the fly.

Man and tsetse cannot live together and where they meet they must join battle, for the tsetse is a killer that spreads sleeping sickness to man and *nagana* to his cattle. Both diseases, unless treated, can be fatal. Yet the tsetse does not carry the disease to the wild animals that are its favourite prey. That is the irony of the 60-year war. Wildlife can share the tsetse's territory in peace; man has got to go.

Until the 1880s the fly infected all the Okavango Delta and all the intervening area north to the Chobe as well. Then in 1896 the rinderpest epidemic swept through southern Africa killing game and cattle until there was no fresh blood to suck and most of the tsetse died too. But there were survivors, and they made a relentless return; 14 metres of new territory a day, almost imperceptible over weeks and months, but counted in years, a slow but sure progression.

By the 1940s the people of the Okavango had been forced as far back as they could go. They had retreated to the last watering-points; behind them lay the desert. A special unit was established and man began skirmishing along the advancing front, first with rifles, mowing down the antelope in the belief that by depriving the tsetse of food, the fly would die. Then, in the belief that without shade in which to breed the fly must surely go, trees were ring-barked and, still standing, died.

Sporadically the war went on until there were 50 baTawana hunters working fulltime killing more than 4 000 animals a year. But man chose a narrow front for his operations – a strip of land west of the town of Maun. Here the tsetse were held, but elsewhere they went on creeping through the bush, claiming new land, unchecked.

In 1967 teams of men with knapsack sprayers used a poison, dieldrin, to clear 9 000 square metres of tsetse country. To an enemy settled safely over 110 000 000 this victory was scant, but it showed that a change of weapon could mark the turning-point of the war.

Recently, aircraft have skimmed the treetops at night spraying droplets of new poison, endosulphan, on the tsetse roosting in the trees.

The aerial attacks remain experimental for the time being while the commanders check their weapon.

However, if the poison does prove 'safe' – do we really want to win the war? Have we the wisdom the rule the dominion of the fly? There are places where man and cattle lived near the Delta for less than 20 years before they were chased by the fly. Yet today, 50 years later, the countryside still bears the scars of that brief occupation.

Nobody wants the tsetse – but if the tsetse go will another desert follow the cattle into the Okavango's wild country?

For more than 600 kilometres our mokoro has led us, and with the flood there has been a choice of many rivers. But now we begin to notice that the islands are falling behind, that the river's gleam has become elusive. The water still sparkles, but it is disappearing beneath us as we move until at last there is no choice, just this one river, unexpectedly straight after the many days of twists and turns.

Sand has no lines, yet from the air there is no doubt about the odd sense of straightness here on the sand mantle. That 'sense of straightness' is a fault, a crack in the earth's crust where Africa is tearing itself apart. It lies more than 200 metres below the surface, yet it has shifted the sands to divert the last of the Okavango's water abruptly north-east and south-west. Towards the end the river carries a mere 2% of the water with which it started at Shakawe. Sun and leaf and root have taken the rest. So we paddle on this slender stream, a transient, luminous remnant of a wide shining waterway we left far behind, so many days and nights behind.

Where did we lose the great river on which we set out? What happened to our Okavango? The journey ends too suddenly on a beach at Maun.

The Pans.

It is a road that drags in the dust, slow and hot and weary. An empty road that meanders into emptiness.

Other roads have always had a certainty, a sense of direction. But this desert road is different. Carelessly it leads you and loses you, a solitary straggler on spaces that drowse in the heat. Sometimes the road disappears for a while, hidden in its own dust, too tired to move. Then it ambles off again meandering round thickets of thorn, seeking diversions on the endless plains of the Kalahari; a dithering road that frightens the stranger with its stops and starts and silences. Yet the road is not as lonely as it seems. Many tracks criss-cross its path or keep it company along the way.

On our first evening, long ago now, as we travelled to Makgadikgadi's pans, a herd of gemsbok raced ahead of us, horns flashing through the grass, and we stopped and scrambled to the roof of our truck to watch them go. Once a crowd of ostrich danced from the darkness, high-kicking their shadows as we made our fire for the night.

Although we have travelled the road many times, no trip was ever quite the same.

On a cold winter morning, a Bushman, wrapped in a mantle of skins, crossed our path on the open plains. We called a greeting, hoping to stop him, but with a glance he kept going, unhurried on his way to the middle of nowhere. Once we woke to see a giraffe cantering across the dawn sky. Hardly a tree grew on all those open horizons, so how had the giraffe come to be there? While we watched, wondering, the animal saw us and veered away, galloping until at last it was out of sight.

For more than 100 years this rambling, haphazard road was man's southern highway to the Okavango, and the road and its travellers stayed alive because their path crept close to a desert river all the way. Maps show clearly how road and river follow one another's twists and turns, but on our first journey it was a long time before we discovered that there was this river, out of sight, quiet in the bush. It was a long time before we reached the shade of tall acacias that look down on the flowing brown water of the beautiful Boteti.

But perhaps only the thirsty wanderers of this desert road, skin and hair stiff with the dust of long, dry days, can really appreciate the loveliness of this river.

'The messenger sent in haste is always forced to spend the night along the way by the abundance you place before him.' So the baYei people sang the praises of their Boteti River.

'A glorious river,' echoed early white travellers. 'The trees which adorn the banks are magnificent,' said one. 'Groves of golden-blossomed mimosa,' declared another. 'A river with reedy margins, lotus leaves and flowers, ravenous crocodiles, screeching, creaking, clamorous flocks of birds . . .'

The Boteti carries the last of the Okavango's water away from the swamps and out across the desert, a narrow river that haunts a channel too deep and too wide for it. But although it may be just a thin ghost of what it was, without the Boteti there would be no life in this interior of Botswana. There would be no scattered villages and trading stores, no wild herds, wheeling in from the desert, no cattle, donkeys and goats, perhaps no diamond mine at Orapa. There would be no highway to the Okavango.

Elephants first pounded the outlines of the road upon the Kalahari sands. For a thousand years their steady processions marched in from the desert to squeal and trumpet in the cool brown water. Rhino blundered after them, and buffalo cantered along the river's edge, crashing down the banks to stand snorting and bellowing in the water, chasing the crocodiles from their pools.

The bare feet of desert people touched the road lightly, toes curling from the hot earth. They knew no other route across the Kalahari and they showed the way to the creaking wagons of the first white explorers. And in this way our road began to acquire a history.

On the first cool evening of autumn, when the first touch of gold is on the grass, there is the sound of hooves returning from the desert, rustling up the winds along the plains.

Once black hunters waited for this sigh of the changing seasons. Then they closed in on the desert's waterfront, weighting spearheads above the paths, stringing up snares where birds and mammals,like criminals, were suspended by the neck; they set traps and dug pits all along the banks of the Boteti and among the seeps at the edge of the Makgadikgadi pans. In the long dry months the herds had to get to water, so they had to run the gauntlet of the waiting hunters. Eland came slowly, hooves clicking, with hundreds of zebra and shaggy wildebeest, with troops of impala and giraffe and buffalo. When the winter months were over their horns and bones littered the hunters' camps among the trees.

In the 1850s white travellers following the river road to the interior discovered the good hunting along the Boteti, and they, too, lingered on the river banks . . . and in the pitfalls.

'The pitfalls are covered with great care,' reported missionary-doctor David Livingstone. 'All the excavated earth is removed to a distance so as not to excite suspicion in the minds of the animals. Reeds and grass are laid across the top; above this sand is thrown and water so as to appear exactly like the rest of the spot. Some of our party plumped into these pitfalls more than once, even when in search of them in order to open them to prevent the loss of our cattle.'

Many early journals ruefully report similar incidents: 'Here four of my brother's oxen had fallen into game pits,' remarked James Chapman on his way to the grasslands of Makgadikgadi. The young adventurer was the first white man to explore these plains where 'the gnus, the quaggas and the springboks were so tame, owing to their ignorance of the gun, and besides so abundant that we did not care to shoot them.' He described how he outspanned beside a pool 'which was all night kept in commotion, the splashing of water, the din of clattering hooves, the lowing and moaning of gnus being mingled in discordant notes. The braying of the quaggas was terrible . . .' Chapman estimated that, over a ten-hour period, 12 000 animals drank at the pool. He was in a hunter's paradise and became casual about his bag which on one day included 'ducks and geese, partridges, doves, a dozen springbok, two gnus, four quaggas and a rhinoceros'.

His carriers were soon so burdened with meat that he refused to let them carry any more and left carcases behind. He wrote: 'The Bushmen turned back to shower maledictions on the vultures for lighting on the flesh. It is beyond their comprehension how we can be so prodigal as not to remain until we have devoured the flesh we kill.'

Chapman travelled during a period of turmoil in Botswana with intertribal strife disrupting the life of the Kalahari people. He was not surprised at breakfast to be interrupted by '200 or 300 Bushmen, women and children flying in breathless haste, carrying their pots and utensils on their heads, occasionally stopping to look around, evidently in great terror.'

The dust of the sleepy highway stirred with the upheavals and then settled again, covering nameless graves. For 20 years loose tracks hardened as messengers came hurrying with news of the marauding party of one tribe, or the advancing commandos of another.

For 20 years there were raids and attacks and skirmishes and when the warfare ceased at last you could just discern the shape of the road, through the trees and over the plain, a route to the Okavango.

And yet the edges of the new highway were easily hidden by the spoor of the wild herds that still moved in every winter, close to the Boteti. With the wars behind them, men had time to listen once more for the return of the zebra and the eland and the springbok. White traders arrived in their wagons to barter with black hunters, to collect the country's harvest of skin and horn, to chase the few elephant left along the Boteti for tusks which were hacked out for the billiard balls, combs, chessmen, piano keys and doorhandles of Europe.

And soon the road had become accustomed not only to wagons, but to the tread of cattle, for the people of the desert were beginning to build up domestic herds with the wealth bought from the wild.

By 1870 change was on its way to Botswana, change more dramatic than the piled trophies at the trading stores. It was the change that lay among the grasses of the Kalahari, change that would touch the history of our road, but 60 years would pass before it would be documented.

And all that time the Boteti kept on flowing, out of sight but close to the highway, a lifeline to travellers, a river ever in search of the sea.

For 600 kilometres the Boteti's brown waters slither through the Kalahari. In dry years it is a river shrivelled by sand, in wet years one which splashes its flood as far as the reed marsh that is Lake Xau or Makgadikgadi's silent lake beyond. You can still see the shoreline of the mysterious Makgadikgadi, although the road skirts it cautiously. Once there was the lapping water of a lake 22 metres deep, now there is just the blinding glitter of salt pans, a 12 000 square kilometre skeleton laid out among ancient lake beds. The lake in prehistoric times was bigger than Lake Victoria and covered most of northern Botswana.

Water has never been known to flow through most of these dusty depressions – in fact no coherent channels remain and they have probably been dry throughout historic time. No one knows whether change of climate killed the system, or whether the change came from movement in the earth's crust that interfered with the river courses. Perhaps the Boteti's channel was carved by another river in another age. There are scientists who believe that only a river the size of the Zambezi could have filled the great lake; that there never was sufficient volume from its present feeders, the Boteti in the south and the Nata River in the north; nor was there ever enough water flowing from the dead riverbeds to create the Makgadikgadi of once-upon-a-time. There is evidence to support these theories and although geologists keep taking measurements and making guesses, the history of Makgadikgadi remains as elusive as the waves that dance in its mirages, as enigmatic as the three granite walls that stand somewhere in the middle of its snow-white dazzle.

The walls are built on a hump, in a horseshoe shape that opens onto the salt pan. Perhaps it was a market-place with defences for unknown traders of long ago, but time has tumbled the rocks. Around the broken walls only baobabs squat in passive solitude.

Makgadikgadi is not always dry. Heavy rains can overnight transform parts of it into shallow blue pans and then, out of the sky, arriving from nowhere, come the circling, settling wings of flamingo, a hundred thousand birds whose harsh clatter creates a brief spectacle on the lake. For weeks the pink shimmer lies on the water – and then, within hours, the unpredictable nomads vanish as suddenly as they came.

In the summer of 1976 the water had dried up and the birds had moved on when Peter Johnson and a pilot friend, flying over Makgadikgadi, noticed movement on a damp patch of mud far below. They circled lower and found that there were 5 000 flamingo chicks, unable to fly but obviously able to walk, for their tiny trail was scratched to the horizon. And some parent birds were visible, too, pink feathers conspicuous among the drab brown colour of the young.

The Pans

Was the nursery trekking to water? It had happened before, at Etosha Pan in Namibia in 1971 when 30 000 flamingo chicks trudged 80 kilometres to water while the parent birds did relays, airlifting food all the way. The plane circled several times above the flamingo column, then, questions still unanswered, it flew on.

Fingers of grass slip inside the shoreline of Makgadikgadi's salts, tentative explorers from the running, blowing grasslands that surround the dead lake. No road has ever penetrated far among the grasses. Neither our old highway that wandered from the south of the pans, nor the newer road built along the north. The grasses swish and crackle across spaces of unending golden sameness. A vantage-point on top of a termite mound adds only further flatness to the view.

You have to take a plane, dodging vultures and bataleur eagles, to get perspective. Only from the air can you see the game trails meandering through the grasses, and the small pans full of waterfowl, and herds of 200, 500, 1 000 wildebeest, and the bursting dust plumes of galloping springbok and gemsbok and zebra. Here and there stunted thornbushes sag with the weight of vulture nests, while bat-eared foxes skitter off termite mounds and ostrich flounce like chorus girls. And wherever you fly there are more animals, and still more animals. Hundreds, and then thousands, and then tens of thousands.

Twenty years earlier there were not tens of thousands but hundreds of thousands of animals blurring the grasses. They began as a few herds of wildebeest gathered near Makgadikgadi's Sua Pan in the 1950s, and their numbers began to build up until within ten years there were 250 000, animal nudging animal, impossible to count. Then, just as suddenly, the wildebeest began to die off until by 1965 there were very few left.

Instability among the grasses has brought disorder to the Kalahari. The great wildebeest crash is a phenomenon typical of when vegetation is in a state of flux. Although the details are poorly understood, Botswana's scientists believe that the wildebeest build-up began when fire and cattle killed certain grasses, allowing others to spread. The new growth was favourable to wildebeest and their numbers temporarily increased until they became so numerous that they destroyed their own food source and starved.

There are signs of chaos in the grass all along the road to the Okavango, although the newcomer must look with searching eyes. Many years before the signs had already been noted by South African botanist I. B. Pole Evans who drove to the Makgadikgadi in 1929. He gave barely a glance to the antelope – or to the antbear holes into which he kept falling. He had eyes only for the grasses along the way, and where he found one clipped short by a grazing animal, he dug it up and took it home to Pretoria to be planted in a pot. There were secrets hidden in these thirstlands and he was after them. For years Botswana had been renowned for her cattle. Even when the animals had been driven 640 kilometres across the desert, they were fat. Somewhere they must feed on wonder grasses.

Excited at the results of his first expedition, he was soon at work persuading the South African Government to finance a second in 1937.

He had some assistants for the second trip, and an official blessing to journey from Makgadikgadi, up the Boteti to the Okavango Delta.

And all along the way, there were the wonder grasses he had dreamed about.

'The *Digitarias* from the desert have shown remarkable growth,' he was to rejoice. In eight weeks individual plants covered 'a space of 500 square feet'. The expedition collected 400 different kinds of grasses, and 15 000 rooted plants were eventually potted out in the Transvaal.

Yet Pole Evans was a deeply troubled man as he pushed his Ford V8 across the sandveld. He knew that the promise of the Kalahari's golden grasses was readily misunderstood for although they were at home on the soft, dry sands of the desert, they were delicate plants, easily shattered. And like all life under the wide desert sky, even the grasses were made for a life of migration.

They were made for the wild herds that moved freely, grazing one year, not returning for several seasons more. In irregular rhythms lay their permanence. But wherever the South African botanist travelled he saw grasses burdened with the regular munch of cattle. Perennials had given way to worthless annuals, annuals had made way for weeds, and then thickets of thornscrub had marched in to invade the sand. Where once there had been reedbeds full of lechwe and sitatunga on the Boteti, now there were dust storms that blew with every wind.

Pole Evans recorded: 'Wherever man had settled for any length of time perennial springs had ceased to flow there, rivers and swamps had dried up, grassland had been converted into thornscrub and thornscrub turned into a veritable desert. All these phases of the destructive influence of man in a semi-arid climate are now to be seen in no unmistakeable manner . . . and to me this was one of the most striking features of the trip.'

His words had little effect on a colonial administration that saw the country's immediate wealth in cattle rather than grass. In 1949 the Colonial Development Corporation set up a cattle-holding station on the open grassland plains north of the Boteti where up to 10 000 cattle were grazed at a time before being trekked to market. For centuries wild herds of antelope had fed in the same areas and the plains had continued to flourish. But the relentless chewing of cattle broke the vigour of the grasses so rapidly that within only 20 years thornbush thickets 30 kilometres wide invaded the plains.

You don't have to be an expert to make your own reading of the state of the countryside. Just drive out into the Botswana night and sooner or later you will come upon the shining eyes of crowds of long-tailed springhares. Like small kangaroos they lollop and bounce and leap in the headlights. Where there is springhare, there is damaged grassland. Not for these creatures leafy perennial pastures, they are only comfortable when the grass is retreating – which is why you will find them at densities of 60 animals a hectare on the bare ground around villages, cattle posts, croplands and along river banks. Soon after dusk they leave their burrows to graze and dig for roots, corms, seeds and tubers, shovelling the food into their mouths with their front paws. Before dawn they are back in their holes, plugging their burrows with dirt before dozing off upright, long tails wrapped neatly around their feet.

The springhare population explosion has had one good result: meat for the cooking pot. More than 2 500 000 are hunted every year, hooked up out of their holes as they sleep. That amounts to four per person in Botswana, meat equal to 20 000 cows – meat worth more than a $1 000 000 a year. And that makes the springhare one of the country's most important sources of protein.

When vegetation is in the process of changing, it often happens that an animal such as the springhare will suddenly benefit and expand its numbers and its area. If the plants continue to change, the animal population can be left behind to crash as suddenly as it grew – as happened to Makgadikgadi's wildebeest.

North along our desert highway stretches a fence – a strange event in an almost fenceless country. Until the 1950s Botswana's people farmed without fences, and the wildlife wandered where it would because there were no barriers to mark this man's land from that. Then in 1957 there was a severe outbreak of foot-and-mouth disease. A year later there was another. Then another and another. Botswana's cattle industry came to a standstill. The people had always turned to wildlife in times of economic crisis and now they did so again, and traders, unable to deal in cattle, were quick to accept wildlife trophies instead. Yet it was not the hunter but the cow that would permanently affect the free-roaming wildlife of the Kalahari.

In the late 1950s the veterinary authorities began to stretch wire across Botswana's vast spaces, permanently dividing the country into four quarantine areas in an attempt to control the outbreaks of foot-and-mouth disease.

By the mid-60s the last wire had been stretched into place and the last gap closed. There was a new companion running next to the desert road and the Boteti River – an impenetrable line called the Kuki fence.

The year before the fences closed researcher George Silberbauer was at work in the central desert, where he recorded that it was 'by no means unique to encounter a mixed herd of gemsbok, eland and hartebeest which covered an area five miles long by three miles wide.' Silberbauer said his area 'abounded in wildebeest, kudu, springbok, giraffe, lion, leopard and cheetah. Hundreds of black-back jackal and bat-eared foxes were to be seen. This last winter I found one brown hyaena, four jackals, 20 foxes, no trace whatsoever of lion, leopard or cheetah, six springboks, a disconsolate wildebeest which almost seemed to welcome my company as relief to his loneliness, and a pair of gemsbok.' Silberbauer's summer count showed that in one year the wildlife had been reduced by 75%. He had no doubt that the Kuki fence was responsible.

The wire strands that separated game from water were obstacles more devastating than the pitfalls and traps and snares of 100 years before. Only when migratory herds began to pile up, dying, at the fences, did anyone realise how sharply the wire had blocked age-old migration routes.

But while the cordon fences prevented movements south and east, there was a vast block of unaffected country to the north which included the Boteti and the plains around Makgadikgadi. Perhaps 'block' is inadequate for a territory the size of Portugal, unfenced and virtually unsettled.

Here the Botswana Government proclaimed two new game reserves, the Nxai Pan National Park and the Makgadikgadi Pans Game Reserve.

Nxai Pan is a 150 square kilometre dead lake-bed scattered with islands of trees. Herds of gemsbok, wildebeest, zebra and springbok congregate here in summer – and in autumn move south to Makgadikgadi's pans and plains, crossing the main road and barring the traveller's way.

The countryside may have changed in 100 years, its vastness may be diminished, but the plains remain a place to lose yourself. No roads cross the vastness so you pick your own path, following the wind or the herd that passed before you, or even chasing the butterflies that flutter past in mass migrations. There is no way to count them. They make a column of wings, metres deep, several kilometres wide, stretching from one skyline to the other, spattering windscreens, clogging the radiator, never diverting from their sure movement north. For days and nights the butterflies fly past.

Sometimes a lone rhino leaves its heavy tracks. Occasionally elephant parties appear on the same long stroll, looming up one day at Nxai, disappearing again the next.

Makgadikgadi's grasslands stretch to the banks of the Boteti where cattle low across the river and donkey bray in argument. So wildlife and man live close together on the river's banks, sharing the waterfront as they have always done.

A cynic once said that the two most lethal animals in Africa were the cow and the veterinary surgeon. When you know the history of the river and the pans and the grasses of the Kalahari, what that cynic said seems very true.

Chobe, Linyanti, Savuti.

The Magwegquana Spillway is the only northern tributary of the Okavango. It moves alone across 120 kilometres, disguised in grass and sedge and reed following the buried line of the Magwegquana Fault, an area of underground agitation in the past, of suspected disquiet now. Only in years of exceptional flood do spurts of water break its seclusion, taking Okavango overflow to the Chobe River. The Magwegquana is the last living link between the two systems, proof of the unbroken waterway that beckoned the first Okavango immigrants 250 years ago.

Man was always just a fleeting visitor to the unbroken savannas which conceal Magwegquana. Hunters closed in on the chase but soon retreated, back to the river country, back to Chobe.

Frederick Courtenay Selous, one of the most famous of the big-game hunters, discovered its hunting grounds in 1874. Travelling up the Chobe River in a fleet of 13 dugout canoes he wrote: '. . . and altogether I never enjoyed any part of my wanderings so much as this canoe trip.'

'The whole country was a sheet of water, interspersed with islands. There was always a cool breeze blowing across these watery wastes, even during the heat of day. In every direction herds of graceful lechwe were to be seen standing about in the shallow water, but they were very shy and would not allow the canoes to approach within shot. Wildfowl, geese, duck, and teal of many kinds abounded and I also noticed several species of bitterns, egrets and ibises and other water-loving birds that I had not seen before; whilst my attention was constantly attracted by the shrill, plaintive cries of large white-headed ospreys as they sailed in graceful circles overhead.'

When elephant were sighted on a remote island one afternoon Selous marvelled: 'Fancy elephants in this age so little disturbed as to drink in the daytime.' Early days . . . and already it was remarkable to see a herd out in the open.

That week Selous killed ten elephant and he was not the first nor the last hunter to sit around a Chobe campfire relishing 'a piece of elephant's heart, nicely salted and peppered, roasting on a forked stick over the coals. The heart is the titbit in my opinion,' he said, 'although some people prefer the foot or trunk. The inside fat, when rendered down, is almost as good as butter.'

Yet hunting among islands which had never heard a gun before, even Selous had some misgivings.

'It seems dreadful to slaughter so many of these huge creatures merely for the sake of their tusks,' he admitted, 'for if there are no Bushmen or natives about the carcases are abandoned to the hyaenas and vultures. But *il faut vivre*. Ivory is the only thing obtainable in this country with which to defray the heavy expenses of hunting and if you depend on your gun for a living as was my case, it behoves you to do your best when you have a chance.' And as he pointed out, sometimes he had to tramp for six weeks without getting anything better than antelope for the supper pot.

The Chobe hunter had to tramp. There was no other way to reach the hunting grounds except on foot, for Chobe was tsetse country. Wrote Selous: 'Hunger, thirst, fatigue and all the other hardships of the elephant hunter sank into insignificance as compared with the unceasing irritation caused by the bites of the tsetse . . .'

So far away, safe on the outskirts of the fly belt, hunters left their wagons and horses and oxen. They filled calabashes with water, slung them on the assegais of their servants, and then set off to follow the spoor they found on the sand.

Chobe, Savuti, Linyanti

Because they went on foot the early hunters left no tracks and even later, when the hunters came by lorry, their tyres just pressed the grasses down to show where they had passed. Many men took the long road north to Chobe, famous men like Selous who wrote the story of his hunts, and other men who kept their adventures to themselves, unknown hunters who came and went with loads of meat and tusks and hides.

'I wore out thirteen barrels shooting crocs,' boasted one oldtimer who spent a lifetime along the river, but he told his tales over drinks with passing strangers. He left no written record of his bag.

Eventually Botswana brought in laws and licences to control the hunting but there was no staff to patrol the wild northern spaces and the poachers knew it and were casual about their shooting trips. They camped openly under trees strung with red meat, and when the sun had dried the venison, they packed it into bags and loaded their lorries for home. Next winter they were back again.

As long as the white men had been hunting, black men had been hunting too, with pits and snares and traps, with jabbing spears and with the loud explosions of ancient muzzle-loaders. And the black men were the first to show concern. On the northern edge of the Okavango there is a place where rivers and lagoons and dry parkland intertwine. Here the baTawana had hunted every winter. But by the 1960s the tribesmen noticed that it was more difficult to hunt. They had to travel further. The animals were fewer and were wary.

At last the tribe met to make a decision: 5 000 square kilometres of traditional baTawana hunting ground would be set aside as the first big wildlife sanctuary in the Okavango, the Moremi Wildlife Reserve.

Soon afterwards the Botswana Government declared the Chobe National Park, 11 700 square kilometres of the country's northern frontier where processions of elephant move back and forth with careless disregard for the international boundary. Tail to trunk they swim across the rivers, or follow the corridors their footprints have built through the bush.

There are no people living in this strange country with its lost savannas and dislocated river channels. Neither by land nor by water can man negotiate with ease the waving green floodplains and the brown waterways of the Kwando-Linyanti-that-becomes-the-Chobe River, a companion to the Okavango as eccentric and peculiar.

The Linyanti, like the Okavango, is an inland delta with islands, streams and shallows. When dry winter dusts settle on the bush only then does the Linyanti come into flood. And then wild animals gather in their thousands, so many that pilots have crashed their aircraft forgetting the controls as they gaze down on the marching elephant, on sandbanks slithering with crocodile, and islands dark with wildebeest, zebra, tsessebe, roan and lazy prides of lion sprawling in the shade.

Along the waterfront troops of baboons pull at waterlily stems like strings of spaghetti and lechwe chase each other in shining trails of flying water.

Down along the riverside is an old hunter's landing strip, rarely used. But when planes swoop low there is a flurry of scarlet wings in the air as the carmine bee-eaters lift off the runway. Linyanti airstrip is the only flat-land colony of these birds, their flashing red wings an incredible spectacle.

The Savuti Channel is an abrupt offshoot of the odd angular Linyanti. It is a temperamental waterway that peters out in the boggy greenery of the Savuti Marsh. It carried water in 1853 and then remained dry for 100 years while huge trees grew along its steep white furrow. In 1957, nobody knows why, Savuti flooded again and the trees drowned and draped their dead limbs over the silky and unexpected water. And ever since, Savuti has remained a place of indecision sometimes so dry that crocodiles are stranded in holes high up in the bank and wildebeest lick desperately at the mud which runs like melted icecream in the last pools; sometimes so wet that elephant swim in the channel and hippo snooze fitfully with fish around their feet.

When Savuti is in flood it becomes a migration focal point and then as far as the eye can see herds of antelope graze among the sedges. Sable, roan, impala, tsessebe, zebra . . . there can be 2 000 animals of more than a dozen species in sight at once. The squelchy bogs are full of whirring, squawking duck parties and breeding snipe intent on display. There are battalions of black buffalo that splosh from the wet greenery of the marshes to the powdery dust of the mopane forest beyond, leaving behind a truculent solitary up to its hocks in mud. When it gets dark they take up a defensive position, backs to the marsh, bleating and bellowing the night hours away. Prides of lion constantly patrol the edge of the bog, panicking the antelope, keeping them moving in their pastures, keeping vultures circling hopefully in the sky.

Yet overnight at Savuti the great herds will disappear, for when the summer rains fall the animals move onto the spaces of dry savanna, wandering among small rainwater pans. Away from the rivers lies this wide forgotten bushveld, where the great herds find sanctuary. On and on it goes. Shadow and light. Tree and sand. Thicket and clearing. Here is a land that belongs to itself.

Lake Ngami.

From the lake shores it looks like a cloud of smoke, tossed by the wind, twisted into spirals in the sky. Then the smoke tumbles in a sunburst of wings, a spinning, flickering tornado that marks the flight of a million birds dispersing from the water's edge. When the quelea are flying it sounds as if rapids have appeared on the placid lake.

Quelea finches are never far from Lake Ngami, cracking the branches of desert trees with the weight of their swarms. They are hard-time birds. Birds of drought. Disaster birds. Sometimes there are millions, sometimes just tens of thousands, yet the quelea are not the only crowds that lift and settle in chattering commotion near the water.

Birds were at Ngami from the beginning, watchers from the sky when the first long ripple hissed across the sand. As the wetness spread and deepened they came down, hovering, fluttering, flapping to the water. Airy long-distance travellers paused up high near the white desert sun, glided and dropped. Pelican and flamingo, ducks and geese, spoonbills and ibis, swifts and swallows – their wings beat the first turbulence on the lake.

The birds knew the lake long before the Bushmen found it, long before baYei hunters stumbled upon it around 1750 and sent word back to the tribe: 'A lake with waves that throw hippo ashore, roaring like thunder. A lake of many, many fish . . . ' And when the baYei heard of it, they left their homeland forever. 'The great lake', it was called. 'The long-looked-for lake', 'the lake of the unknown region', or simply, 'the lake'.

In Victorian drawing-rooms in London the name was repeated; around African campfires and in tribal kraals it was echoed too. Lake Ngami. Legendary Lake Ngami.

For more than 200 years it has called men to its shores, tugging them with dreams and promises. It is the only Okavango lake, outflung on the western base of the Delta, a glittering corner that man cannot leave alone.

There was always only one way to find it – across the desert. The Kalahari covered all tracks to the lake, north, south, east and west, and perhaps in this inaccessibility lay its glamour. From rumour and report men were certain it was there – but they had no way of reaching it to be sure.

Lake Ngami, in its isolation, was peaceful until the 1820s when a new tribe arrived, aggressive baTawana who staked their claim and drove their cattle, sheep and goats to the waterside. They soon became dominant in the area, demanding tribute of meat, skins, plants, corn and even canoes from the gentle baYei, the baKgalagari and the Bushmen. Later the tribute would include ivory and ostrich feathers as well.

The baTawana settled close to Ngami in a village with several hundred huts and they were there on the afternoon of August 1, 1849 when W. C. Oswell, David Livingstone and a Mr Murray became the first white men to behold 'this fine-looking sheet of water'.

It is unlikely that Ngami was all they had expected it to be. Certainly they had known wilder places with fewer people, for the secret lake of legend when they discovered it had baTawana and their stock along its shores and baYei fishing in the shallows. But the wild country still lay close by, and there were almost daily hunts that kept the people's cooking pots full of venison.

Livingstone and company made their way to the baTawana village to introduce themselves to the

20-year-old chief, Letsholathebe, and to ask if there were any goats or oxen to purchase. The chief offered them elephant tusks.

'No, we cannot eat these,' they protested. 'We want something to fill our stomachs.'

'Neither can I eat them,' replied Letsholathebe, 'but I hear you white men are very fond of these bones so I offer them. I want to put the goats in my own stomach.'

Livingstone's trip was brief but well-publicized and the world quickly learnt the news: Lake Ngami had been discovered and ivory was plentiful. Over the next 30 years more than 80 visitors would take their slow ponderous wagons in search of the fabled lake. There were hunters, traders, missionaries, engineers, naturalists – even honeymooners. All were plagued by misfortune: two were eaten by crocodiles, one killed by elephant, two died lost in the bush, one went crazy and at least five succumbed to 'fever'.

The odd straggly invasion made Ngami into a crank's corner. Men came after ivory, after adventure and after souls, and they turned life upside down at the lake, bargaining and bribing, arguing and threatening, preaching and praying.

When Charles Andersson arrived from Walvis Bay in 1853, he wrote: 'To make a favourable impression on the minds of the savages at the first interview . . . I donned my best apparel, which consisted of jacket and trousers of fine white duck, a handsome red velvet sash, lined with silk of the same colour, and a gold embroidered skull cap. The last two articles of dress were a memento of a dear female friend and I had pledged myself to wear them on the first *grand* occasion.'

How did the grandeur strike the tribesmen? Andersson sadly recorded reactions of mirth and ridicule: 'They laugh at us for putting our legs and arms into bags,' he said, 'and for using buttons for the purpose of fastening bandages around our bodies instead of suspending them as ornaments from the neck or hair . . .'

The man most amused of all was the Chief, Letsholathebe, who had a lively and uninhibited sense of humour which he readily enjoyed at his visitors' expense.

'Out of business hours he was an exceedingly pleasant and jocular fellow,' said one trader. But he was also 'uncivilized', 'treacherous', 'villainous', and 'insulting', or so the white people muttered bitterly when they did not get their way. Yet why should they? Letsholathebe did not need an education to make him aware that these people came to his country because they hoped to find a fortune there. He became an astute trader. 'Beads?' he told Andersson. 'We have more than enough. Already the women grunt under their burdens (of beads) like pigs.'

What Letsholathebe wanted were firearms and cows; he and his people would readily exchange ivory for cattle.

Within three years of the white man's discovery of Ngami, 900 elephants had been killed near the lake and instead of their trumpeting in the night there was the lowing of cattle and the bleating of goats. Wildlife became wary of the gun and scattered, while the baTawana's flocks and herds steadily increased. But although the domestic animals were to affect Ngami's history, they were not the only reason why the lake began to change.

Far to the north in the Okavango abandoned rafts had piled up and taken root, becoming papyrus blockages that were squeezing the throat of the Thaoge River that fed Ngami. Within 30 years this main channel of the Delta would be so overgrown with plants that the river would be strangled to death and the lake would gradually choke too.

'Those who have a desire to visit the lake had better be quick about it otherwise they will arrive to see a dry one,' quoted F. Green, a disappointed Ngami traveller in 1855.

But not everybody was disappointed by the dying lake, for in Africa crowds always gather when death is near. Man, hyaena, vulture or fly – singly or in company – they gather for the pickings. And the crowds were assembled at Ngami when trader James Chapman reached the lake in 1853. 'I was astonished to see the number of waterfowl that swarmed over the surface, or moved overhead in clouds that for some moments literally obscured the sun,' he observed. 'As the lake is receding, the fish become plentiful, and waterfowl of every description flock hither from great distances to regale themselves on the fish. Ducks, geese, muscovies, pelicans, flamingoes, herons, cranes, gulls, waterhens, rails, snipe, a species of fish eagle and many other kinds crossed each other on the surface making a deafening noise, and immense crocodiles lay floating within a few feet of the women who dip their vessels for water . . .'

Chapman believed that during the winter months the crocs lay in a state of torpor 'which gives rise to a notion entertained by the natives that their teeth are blunt in winter at which time you may risk a plunge in the water with impunity. But that this is an error was shown by the sad fate of a Mr Robinson who lost his life at this season and at just this spot a year or two ago while waist-deep in pursuit of a couple of ducks he had shot. He was snapped up in the presence of his companion, Mr Moyle, who saw him disappear with a fearful shriek . . .'

Mr Robinson was foolish to rely on blunted teeth, although the African belief had some factual foundation. Cold weather slows down a reptile's metabolism so that it is seldom in need of food during the winter months, saving most – but not all – of its appetite for the summer. Ngami's travellers were wise to be cautious of the crocodiles, but Chapman went into the attack.

'The women at first believing I was shooting birds were delighted and wished to have some; but becoming acquainted with the fact that I was shooting at the crocodiles I received such a torrent of abuse from both sides of the river as I have never been subjected to before or since – such original, scornful, malicious curses as the Bechuana women (who are well-known adepts at this line) alone could invent. They swore that if I molested the crocodiles, which they call Morimo (God) or lion-of-the-water, the river would dry up and they wished me all manner of evil deaths for attacking the evil brutes.'

Saving the crocodiles, however, could not save the people nor Ngami from the bad times that were ahead.

In 1853 the Makololo swept down on the lakeside and drove off most of the baTawana cattle. Then came a continuing drought. The lake already deprived of water by the Thaoge blockages, shrivelled even further into its bed leaving warm, stagnant pools stranded among the reeds and here mosquitoes found ideal breeding conditions. The malaria epidemic that followed killed many people in the reed-walled huts.

'Nothing can be more startling and doleful than the midnight wail of several hundred (mourning) women, and we were often disturbed by them in the few intervals of repose that we managed to steal from the tortures inflicted by the myriads of mosquitoes which visited us nightly,' said Chapman. 'Their numbers are so overwhelming that there is no escape . . . Often we have locked ourselves in a small hut and steamed ourselves in the smoke of cattle dung almost to suffocation without relief.'

And still the misfortunes of the Ngami people were not at an end. A plague of pilferers came from the desert, swarms and swarms of quelea, countless thousands of hungry birds. The drought had withered the desert grasses and without the seedheads on which they depended for food, the birds descended on the crops and demolished the grain of Ngamiland.

And all the while the spluttering Thaoge fed less and less water into Ngami until in 1896 the river was finally stifled in papyrus and Ngami fell silent in a wide hollow grave. What happened to the hippo that once thundered in the lake? Were they all hunted or did they retreat in time to the Okavango? What happened to the crocodiles? Did they migrate to the Okavango too? And the fish? Were they caught and eaten before Ngami died in its last puddle? There is no way of knowing.

We can guess that the birds were careless defectors, feathered gangs of freebooters that took what they could and then soared away to look for other waters. They had no ties to keep them at Ngami. And the wild animals had this freedom too. Wandering the Kalahari, they did not have to have a waterhole. Gemsbok, eland, kudu, springbok and giraffe could get the moisture they needed from browsing, from dew, from bulbs and melons, even from grass so dry that by day it crumbled into powder at the touch. But desert grasses absorb the brief humidity of the desert night, and for this reason many animals do their feeding in the dark. Lion, leopard, cheetah and wild dog sometimes crouched quietly to lap along Ngami's shore, but with moisture from their prey, they too could live without the lake.

Only cattle were captive to the waterhole; they had to drink every day, never far from Ngami's waterfront, and they trampled and grazed the same ground until it was so bare that it looked as if it had been struck by some catastrophe and devastated.

Originally man had been drawn to Ngami because it offered him the best of both worlds, desert and waterway, Kalahari and Okavango, yet it seems he stayed 200 years and never learnt the subtleties of either. He saw that the Kalahari was a place of plenty, of many wild herds, and he thought that this meant his cattle would be plentiful too. When the grass disappeared there were tensions and bitter arguments among the cattle people, groups were split and separated by dissension.

In their first 100 years in Ngamiland the baTawana moved their village capital nines times – but never far from Ngami and the edge of the Okavango. Never far from water.

The baTawana were to remember 1896 for more than the death of the lake. Disasters followed one upon another. First came the locusts. Then rinderpest arrived to wipe out the cattle. The carcases lay heaped on the plains and the vultures became so engorged they were too bloated to fly. The children had sport grabbing the vultures' wings and trying to swing them up for take-off.

After that for more than 50 years Ngami was forgotten.

Then one day in 1953 a slow ripple of water entered the shallow desert depression once more. And birds followed, cruising above the flood, watching for the first flat pools before they whiffled down. Ngami had not died forever.

And the cattle followed the birds, 20 000 animals that came to cool off along the 120 kilometre shoreline, drinking chin-deep, dropping their dung in the water. A hot sun warmed the shallows, blending the dung and rotting vegetation, providing the nutrients for a rich bloom of algae, phytoplankton. Ngami took on the colour of turgid pea soup.

The flood carried fish with it, but these were fish that belonged to the crystal Okavango waterways and most of them disappeared in Ngami's murky soup. But two plankton feeders flourished, the three-spot bream and the green-headed bream. And there was one predator quite at home in the soupy waters, the barbel, a fish so omnivorous that it soon discovered a new source of food – raw cowdung.

Soup and fish – once more Ngami had become a paradise for birds.

We were among the latecomers at Ngami, Peter Johnson being the first of us to visit, in the 1950s flying in a small plane down through flocks of birds, scattering flamingo, waiting while black children chased marabou storks off the landing strip. Out on the lake his boat clanked as it hit masses of fish below, and flocks of terns and gulls screamed overhead, ducking to grab bits of fish chopped up by the churning blade of the propellor.

On a sandspit he counted 5 000 nesting pelicans packed tight, ululating and growling at the boatmen who approached them. Before their breeding was completed the pelicans' sandspit had become a peninsula in a shallower lake and cattle trampled the nests as they grazed among the birds. Only a few hundred nestlings survived.

A shallower lake . . . Ngami was repeating itself and drying up again. In the 1960s a severe drought hit Botswana and 435 000 cattle died, a third of the national herd. Although they were in reach of water, cattle died on Ngami's shores, too. Cattle had to eat as well as drink and in the drought Ngami's overtaxed pastures showed their frailty. Vultures fought over the dead and dying animals, with ruffian bands of bare-necked marabou storks, gobbling rotted flesh.

The drought did not affect the fish, however, and in the soupy waters they were so plentiful that a company was started to harvest the bounty. And then Ngami dried up completely.

The lake has perhaps died many times, but the effort of each brief revival leaves it exhausted, slow-pulsed and feeble.

There is water at Ngami now and there is a lot to see. At a small fishing village on the shores marabou storks queue up next to the offal pits to peck at decayed fish heads and entrails. Swallows and swifts and bee-eaters chase clouds of insects that buzz in the stinking pits. Pratincoles and pippits feed on insects closer to the ground, while barbel skulls give larks a vantage point to survey the plain for small hoppers.

From the lake come the booms and screeches, the whistles and far-carrying cries of thousands of waterbirds. Nomads and vagabonds and adventurers . . . they lift off and desert Ngami when it no longer has what they need. But now there are rafts and skeins and clouds of birds. Loners sail above the lake, eagle and falcon, waiting for a dashing swoop among the doves and finches. There are mobs of teal, up-ended in the water, and ruff and sandpiper, transcontinental migrants, probing the muddy edges of the shores. And there is the distant surge of quelea, twisted like spirals in the sky.

Now for a little while at least, while there is water, Ngami is a spectacle of birds.

Yet Ngami is far-removed from its Okavango parent. It has no clear water, no beds of sedge and reed. It has no fringing forest, no hippo and no crocodile. Nowhere else has man hugged the Okavango so close for so long, and the changes that have come to the lake say much about the fragile relationship between the desert and the nearby Delta. The grasses, quite as much as the water, dictate the rules, although 100 years of disaster has not taught the lesson yet.

At Ngami it is now too late for learning; it must remain forever the Okavango's outcast lake.

Dreams.

The Okavango is one of the few unexploited water-surfaces in Africa and many dreams are wound around it. There are pipe dreams and pump dreams, engineering abracadabras that promise a hey presto! – and the water will be in Rakops or Francistown or Pretoria.

If only it could be switched on and off, while we hold a bowl beneath to gather what we need. If only we could use all that 'wasted' water we could grow cities and factories and make a desert bloom. We could grow rice and we could grow cattle.

Is there a moral somewhere – or is it simply irony – that in trying to manipulate the Delta we have been out-manoeuvred by a plant and bettered by a termite?

Can we ever wrest the Okavango from the plants? If we mow down the papyrus will there really be more water to spare? Will we ever know enough to handle a delta so unstable that a cow, an earthquake, a hippo, a politician – even grains of sand – could change it all? For the Okavango does not belong to Botswana alone. It belongs first to the pastoralist in Angola, to his herds of cattle in the highlands, to the dreams of his leaders, and the leaders of Namibia, too. Can anyone control these dreams?

And the Okavango belongs to Motswadira Kelapile, at this moment punting his family up a river, in a mokoro lowslung with the weight of blankets and nets and pots and pans, the bundles of dried meat, the kaross, the new baby. All they have in the world is piled in this weathered, waterborne, hollowed-out tree trunk.

Once Motswadira went to Gauberg (Johannesburg), the golden city of the mines, where they couldn't pronounce his name so they called him 'Dickson', and they gave him money, but he didn't stay. He had been too long with river freedoms.

In 1976, 80 experts gathered from far corners of the earth for a symposium on the Okavango, on the many dreams and schemes and studies completed or underway.

'The Okavango Delta is a huge natural resource but its economic potential is not as great as many people imagine,' said Keith Thompson, summing up. 'Deltas are very difficult systems to develop successfully. They are complex and they are fragile and many mistakes have been made in the past. Man's technology is nowhere good enough to approach the efficiency of a natural swamp ecosystem. The Okavango Delta has evolved over thousands of years and conserves its resources of water and nutrients more efficiently than could be done by any system with which it could conceivably be replaced. The Delta should not be pushed to produce more than it can reasonably be expected to.

'It is like a reflection in a pool. If you try to get at it, it will disappear altogether. Botswana will need the Okavango Delta in the distant future as much as it needs it now.'

The River:

From a subterranean somewhere flows the source of all existence.

6

5 Constant themes on the Okavango River; water, papyrus, birds, mokoro and man.

6 Awash with the almost surreal colours reflected from a sunset sky the waters of the Okavango slip gently over the kilometre-wide Popa Falls in Kavango, Namibia. The river will never meet rock again for ahead lie only the deep and sapping sands of the Kalahari.

7 On a midstream rock a young Mbukushu woman takes her evening bath.

9

10

8 *Bonga, Xhi, Bakarakwe, Xangtsaudi, Kwadau, Wonga, Xwega, Qaoga* and *Xunxu* . . . the Bushmen have no single name for the Okavango where it begins its slow meanders over the Kalahari sand. Although most of the flow follows the sweeps and coils of the main channel, this aerial view is misleading for the floodplain is waist-deep in water hidden by reeds.

9 The ultimate value of a crocodile lies not in his bellyhide, nor in his value as a tourist attraction, nor even in his ecological significance, but simply in the fact that he is a crocodile, big and ancient and monstrously magnificent.

10 Wise and watchful, a crocodile lies in wait for the herd of goats that comes daily to drink in its territory. Canny creature, the crocodile soon learns the times different animals in the area come to water – and acts accordingly.

11-14 A splash, a bleat of terror – then silence. It is all over within seconds. Using its massive tail as a counterweight the crocodile lunges from the water and grabs a startled goat from the bank. Then, amid silent ripples, the crocodile submerges to drown its victim before beginning its slow underwater meal. What cannot be consumed in one sitting will be stored somewhere under the riverbank until later.

11-14

16

15 At every turn of the river we found a sandbank where great flocks of birds gathered together. Here sacred ibis, white pelican, spoon-bills, wood storks and egrets delight the eye as they scatter downstream.

16 From a bobbing perch above the Okavango a white-fronted bee-eater waits to make a meal of passing dragonflies, butterflies, bees and other insects.

17

17 Frogs in their thousands fill the Okavango night with their delicate tinkling reminiscent of the sound of Chinese windchimes. By day these diminutive (2,5 cm) trapeze artists cling to the river vegetation as they hunt for mosquitoes and other insects.

18 Deep and sonorous, the mating call of the male toad provides a fine bass section to the Okavango River's nightly orchestra. Peering at the world from beneath a lily pad, this toad patiently waits for its twilight feeding time.

18

19

19 Stealing a moment from herding the cattle, a Mbukushu boy cools off in a river pool. Already he is part of a changing society, for when he is an adult he will have to seek employment away from his river home and will perhaps join the many others who travel to the distant gold mines of South Africa to find work.

20

21 22

20 Downstream from Shakawe we came upon these women fishing with baskets made from reeds. This method of fishing is traditionally the work of women and they were obviously enjoying this communal outing as a chance to gossip and have fun.

21 Side by side, the women placed their baskets open-ended to catch the fish that other women upstream chased towards them.

22 This mother playfully offered a small bream to her shoulder-slung infant. While the mother fished, the baby, gurgling with delight, often found itself dunked under the water.

23 Only moments before we had watched as this fish eagle flashed down towards the water in a breathtaking stoop to snatch up a tiger fish from near the surface. The wild, piercing scream of this magnificent predator is heard wherever there is open water in the Okavango.

24 A lone hippo surges ashore. No longer do great companies of hippo snore and wallow among the reeds, but we still found them singly or together in small family parties lurking down quiet inlets. Many river travellers have lost their dugouts and even their lives to those massive jaws.

24

23

25-31 Taxi, fishing boat, carrier of all manner of goods from reeds to pots and pans and trussed up chickens and goats, a mokoro begins its life as a tall hardwood tree chosen for its straightness and unblemished timber. With supreme artistry of the adze, Kay Dumile, his son Dinyando and a colleague shape a canoe in the living trunk. Kay is a master craftsman who learnt his profession from his father, just as he is now passing on his skills to his own son. For two and a half weeks we watched and waited as they hollowed out the trunk of the tree, chopping and trimming and smoothing the wood until the body of our mokoro was an almost uniform five centimetres thick. And as they worked the colour of the wood changed from pristine white when freshly cut to a rich pink and then red until at last there was our vessel, ready for a proud Dinyando to take on her maiden voyage on a peaceful backwater.

32

33

32, 33, 34 Cowboys of the Okavango use mekoro (dugouts) to drive cattle across the river near Shakawe where it is 400 metres wide and a mere two metres deep. Here neighbours lend a helping hand in leading a herd to better grazing on the other bank.

34

36

35

37

38

35 Fire is a permanent feature of the Okavango landscape, scarring vast areas of the floodplain and forest each year. Hunters set the swamps alight to flush out game, and cattlemen, too, put fire to the reeds and papyrus to encourage the new green shoots for their cattle. But some fires appear to start on their own, exploding spontaneously in decaying vegetation. While distant flames ravage a papyrus bed, cattle rest on the short grasses of the floodplain.

36 Green as it may be, papyrus burns with amazing vigour once alight, the flowering heads crackling and popping in the heat as the fire engulfs them with a roar that can be heard for hundreds of metres.

37, 38 The aftermath. Burned alive, this mother crocodile was too late in moving off her riverbank nest to seek refuge from the rapidly advancing inferno. But from her death sprang life for the thousands of bluebottle flies (38) we found newly-hatched from her charred carcase.

40

39 Imbued with abstract qualities from the air, Sepopa – a typical Okavango village – catches the last rays of the afternoon sun. Thatched roofs and reed walls give coolness and privacy to homesteads clustered on the hot desert sand.

40 Through eyes that have watched the Okavango over a lifetime, headman Makoko Moyo of Mohembo sees the slow but certain changes that have come to his woodland world along the great river.

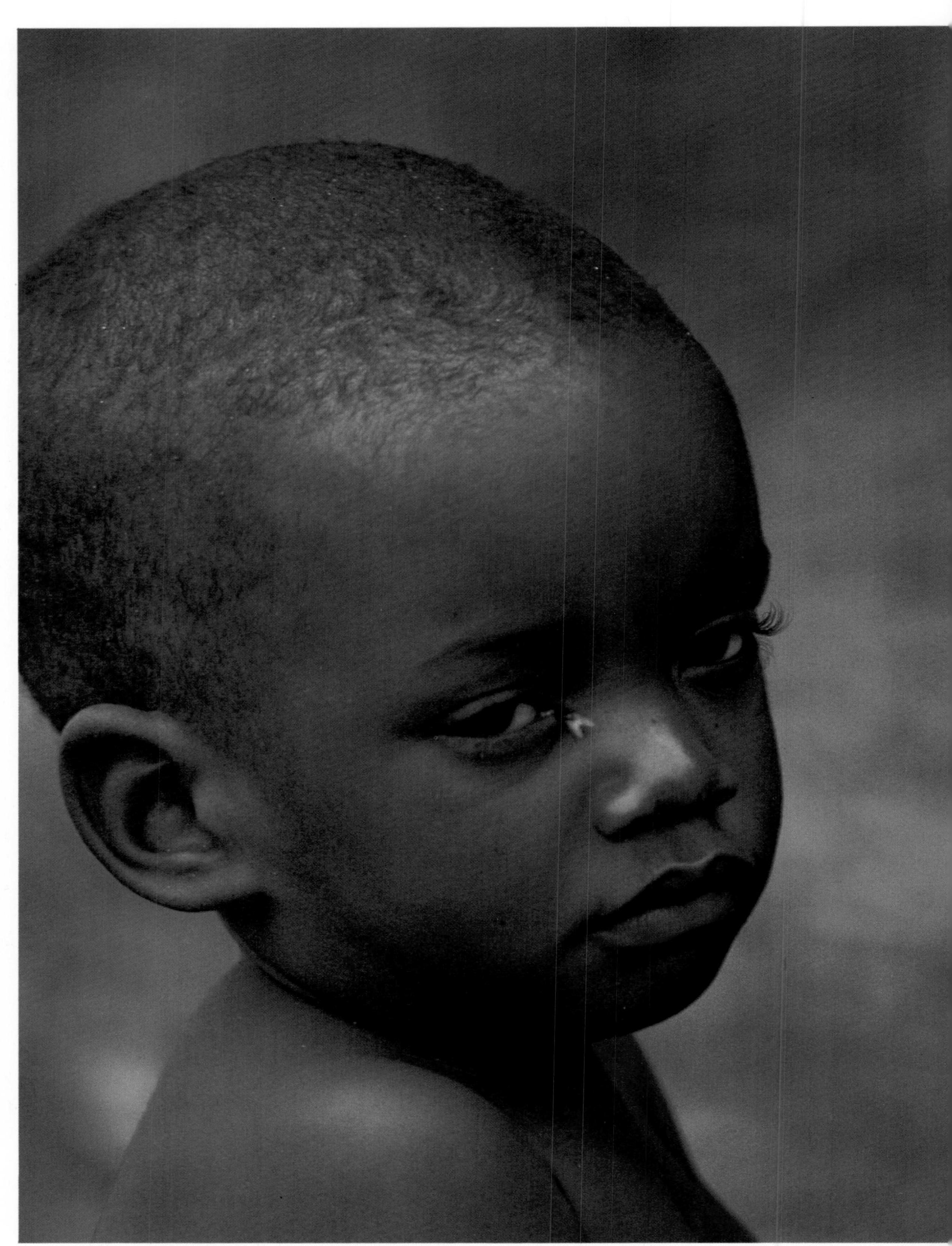

41 We met this mother and child resting at the roadside. She was walking from Mohembo to her father's village more than 100 kilometres away to show her firstborn to her family.

42 Perched on a root projecting from an eroded riverbank, a tiny malachite kingfisher surveys the river for a quick meal.

43 Delicately etched by the last rays of the sun, an African skimmer heads homeward to a sandbank along the river. The skimmer's specially adapted vision allows it to watch where it is going while at the same time it scans the water below for a possible meal. The extended and flattened lower mandible is equally highly evolved. As the bird flies low over the water to feed, its bill just skims the surface and as soon as it touches a fish an automatic reflex is triggered and the bill snaps shut instantly about its prey.

44 A riverside fisherman sports jaunty attire – his hat quite possibly the ceremonial headgear of a long-departed District Commissioner.

45 While fishing with traps is largely left to the women, nets are the province of the men. In the entrances to backwaters and quiet channels villagers put out their nets in the evenings and at dawn return to collect the night's catch.

46 A 30 centimetre-long bream caught in a fisherman's gill net awaits the morrow's cooking pot.

45

The upper reaches of the Okavango are rich in fish, including species such as tiger fish, barbel and squeaker.

47 This old River Bushman, carrying a harpoon, nets and his catch for the day, gazed silently at us as he made his way homeward along a floodplain. Although the River Bushmen or baNoka were the original people of the Okavango, most of them have been assimilated with the black peoples who arrived later in the area.

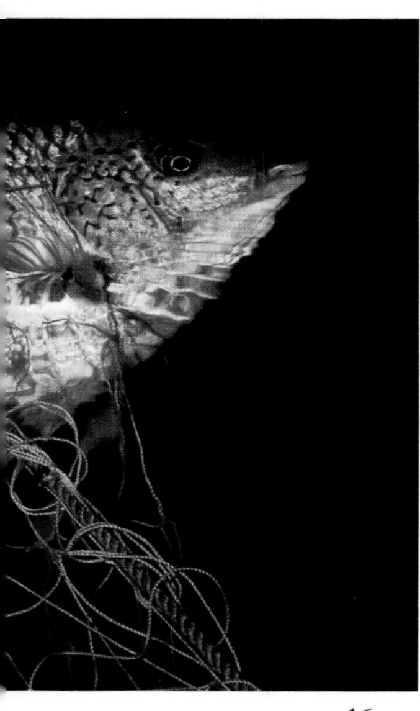

46

47

48

48, 49, 50 For thousands of years the Bushmen have roamed across the spaces of the Kalahari, small bands of desert people at one with their world, hunting and gathering wild food. Although they are wanderers, these !Kung Bushmen distrust unknown territory. 'We do not know how to find food in this country,' they say when in an unfamiliar place. There have been Bushmen near the Tsodilo Hills (50) for centuries, drawn by its seeps and springs and by the strangeness of this lone massif in north-western Botswana. Modern Bushmen do not know the origins of the Bushmen paintings on Tsodilo's cliffs (49), although they were probably made by ancestors of the present !Kung.

50

49

51

51 The almost mystical qualities of Bushman dances are enhanced by the glorious falsetto voices of the women, their staccato hand-clapping and the glowing light cast by the evening fire. The women sit in a tight group around which the men perform ritual dances that reflect the many dimensions of their culture.

52 The Bushman's nomadic way of life that denies him the luxury of many possessions has led to the belief that he is technologically impoverished. Yet if one recognises that for the Bushman the success of the hunt, his knowledge of desert plants as food, and his unerring memory for places that promise water are all vital to his survival, then one must also acknowledge his highly specialised technology. For instance, the hunter's arrow is designed in such a way that once the missile has found its target, the poisoned part of the haft – the part immediately behind the arrow point – comes away from the main body of the weapon so that the animal cannot dislodge the deadly tip.

53 This arrow is designed not to inflict a mortal wound but to carry poison into the bloodstream thereby ensuring a slow but certain death. The poison used comes primarily from the larvae of beetles; the grub of the *Diamphidia* beetle is shown here being squeezed directly onto the sinew and gummed portion behind the arrowhead.

54 Bushmen making fire in the time-honoured fashion.

55 A Bushman near Tsodilo Hills. The band depends for its food on the skills of its hunters and on the *veldkos* (wild foods) collected by the women who can tell by the merest whisp of a dried-out vine whether an edible corm or tuber lies beneath the sandy surface.

52

53

54

55

56 We came quite by chance upon this small band of Bushmen camped below the Tsodilo Hills. They had set up their *scherms* of saplings and straw and intended enjoying for a while the water and good hunting of the place. There are still free roaming Bushmen in Botswana although most of the bands have now become settled around permanent watering-places. As a result many are losing the values and skills needed in an environment that is precarious at best and requires as its first rules of survival, mobility and an intimate knowledge of nature.

57 A bush squirrel gives its cheeky alarm call as two Bushmen set off to hunt in the woodland on the slopes of Tsodilo.

56

57

58

58 Armed only with quivers of poison-tipped arrows, tightly strung bows and their deep empathy with the very creatures they hunt, these two Bushmen are well-equipped to succeed.

59 Lichens, their brilliance created from an alga and fungus living in close mutual association, glow on the rock faces of the Tsodilo Hills.

60 The ever-graceful kudu is a common sight over much of the Okavango area – including Tsodilo's thickets. These antelope provide the Bushmen with food and clothing.

61 Expertly thrusting and twisting his five-metre long stick down a springhare burrow a !Kung Bushman tries to secure a grip on the animal's fur. These kangaroo-like rodents weigh up to three kilograms and make fine eating.

59 60

61

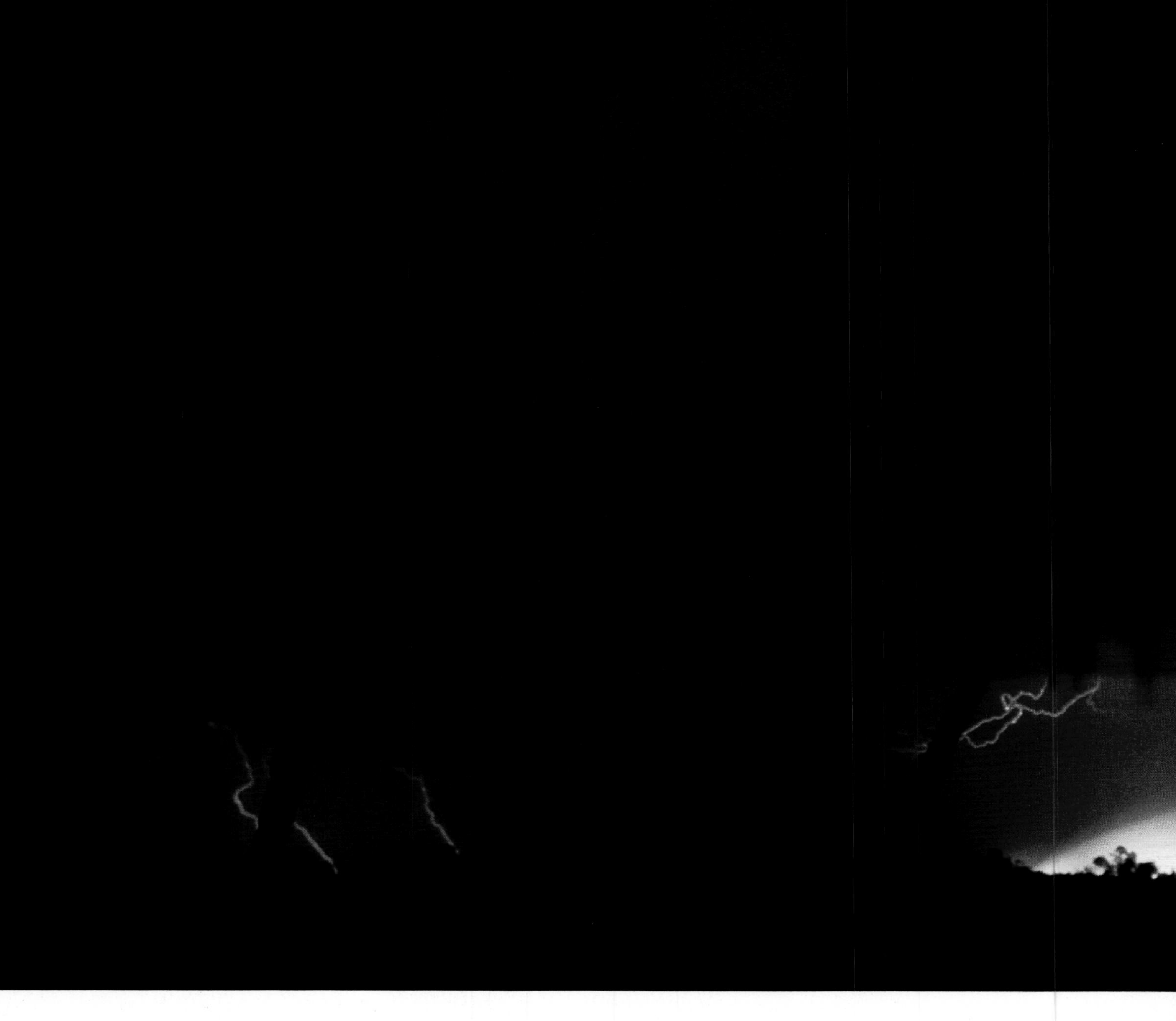

62 As a distant fire rages through floating beds of papyrus, and wild date palms sway in the storm winds, a summer thunderstorm adds its water to the floodlands of the Okavango.

63, 64 Once regarded as a 'rare and elusive bird', the fishing owl can in fact usually be seen by anyone with the stamina and inclination to spend the night looking for it among the trees that overhang the backwaters and lagoons of the Okavango. From its vantage-point this bird locates surfacing fish with its enormous light-sensitive eyes that pinpoint the victim and then swoops down with outsize talons to make its kill.

65 For ten cents or a piece of dried meat or even a length of string, an Okavango ferryman will take you across the river – provided there are no hippo about. All mekoro leak slightly so a wet behind is included in the fare. But for the many ferries operating across the river, the people on either bank would scarcely know each other.

62

63

64

The Delta:

Where the river dies in the desert a paradise is born.

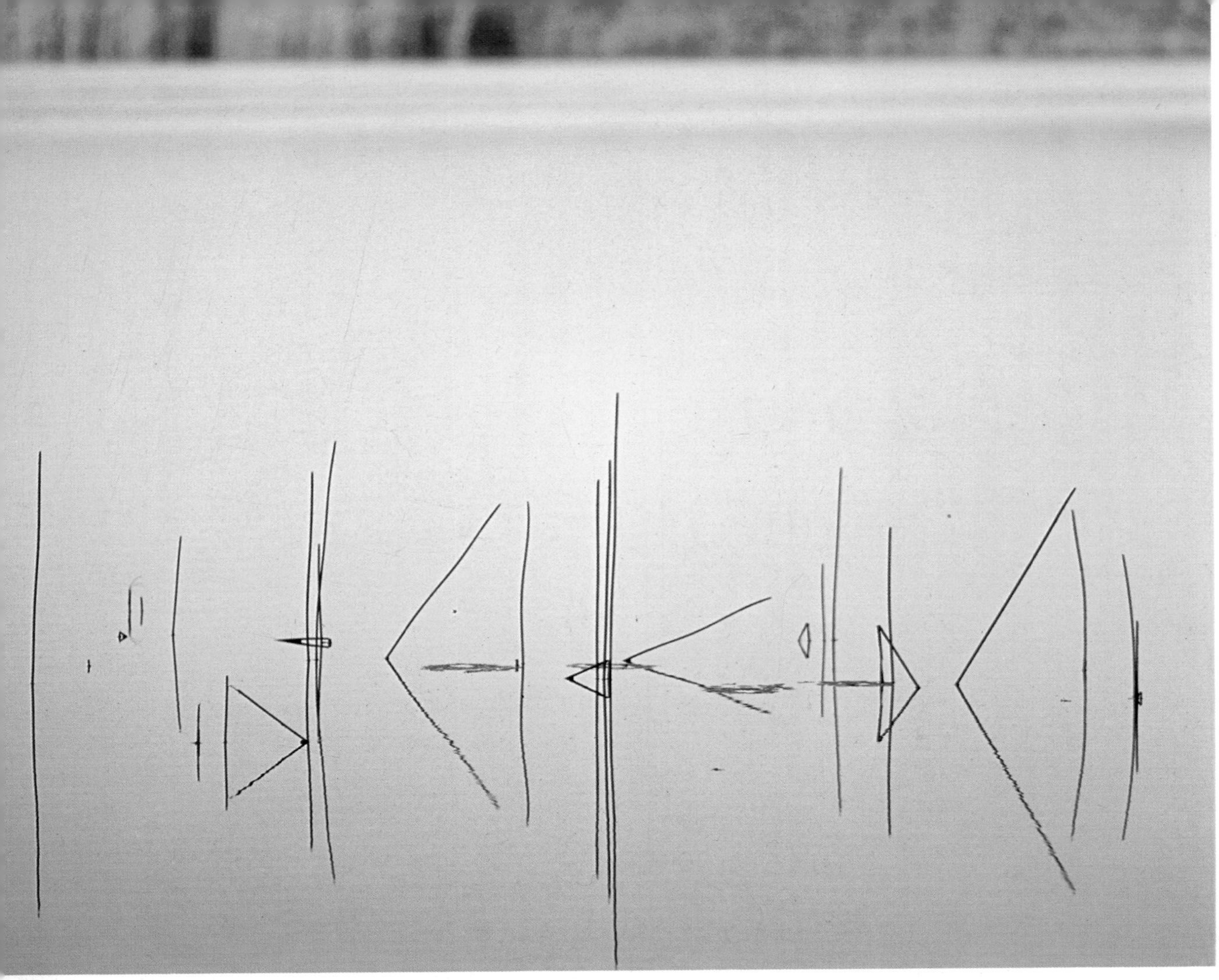

67

66 As it loses its vigour so the Okavango takes on a new beauty, its lazy waters gradually fanning out over the vast flatness of the deep Kalahari sand. And here, among tree-fringed islands and channels waving with sedge and reed, the Okavango spreads out to form one of the greatest inland deltas in the world.

67 Sedge elegantly etched against sunset waters of the Gcobega Lagoon in the north of the Delta.

68 Pulsating beneath the surface of the lagoon tiny (2 cm diameter) jellyfish trap minute water creatures in their stinging tentacles.

69 Often in the Delta we had nothing but the trailing waterlily stems to tell us the direction of the waterflow. While we sometimes chose our path along hippo-cleared channels such as this one, much of the water of the Delta flows through the immense beds of vegetation outside of these well-defined waterways.

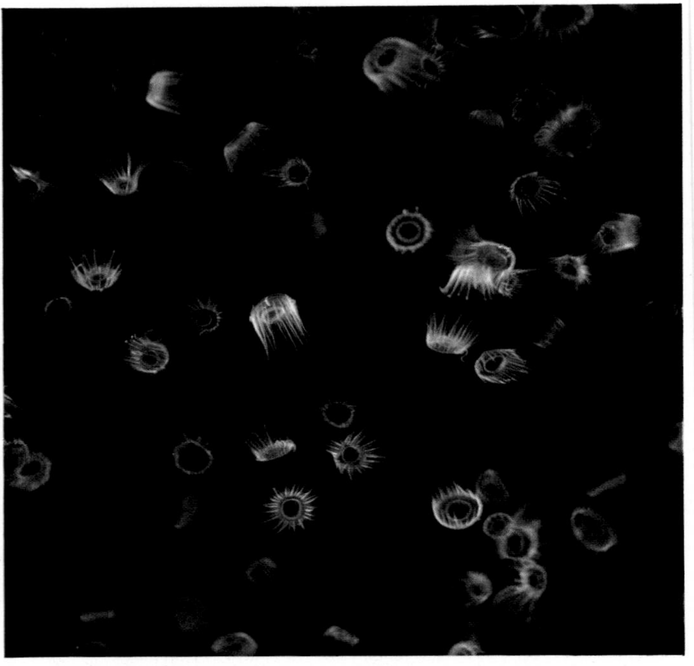

68

70

70 The shy sitatunga seldom ventures far from the floating papyrus beds that are its natural habitat. This antelope is perfectly at home in the water, swimming well and when threatened submerging all but its snout in water. Equipped with extraordinarily long and supple hooves the sitatunga is able to cross floating papyrus with ease – a nightmarish undertaking for man.

71 On a secluded island in the Okavango greenery a pair of male sitatunga lie up in the warm sun, waiting for darkness before they move into the swamp to feed.

71

72

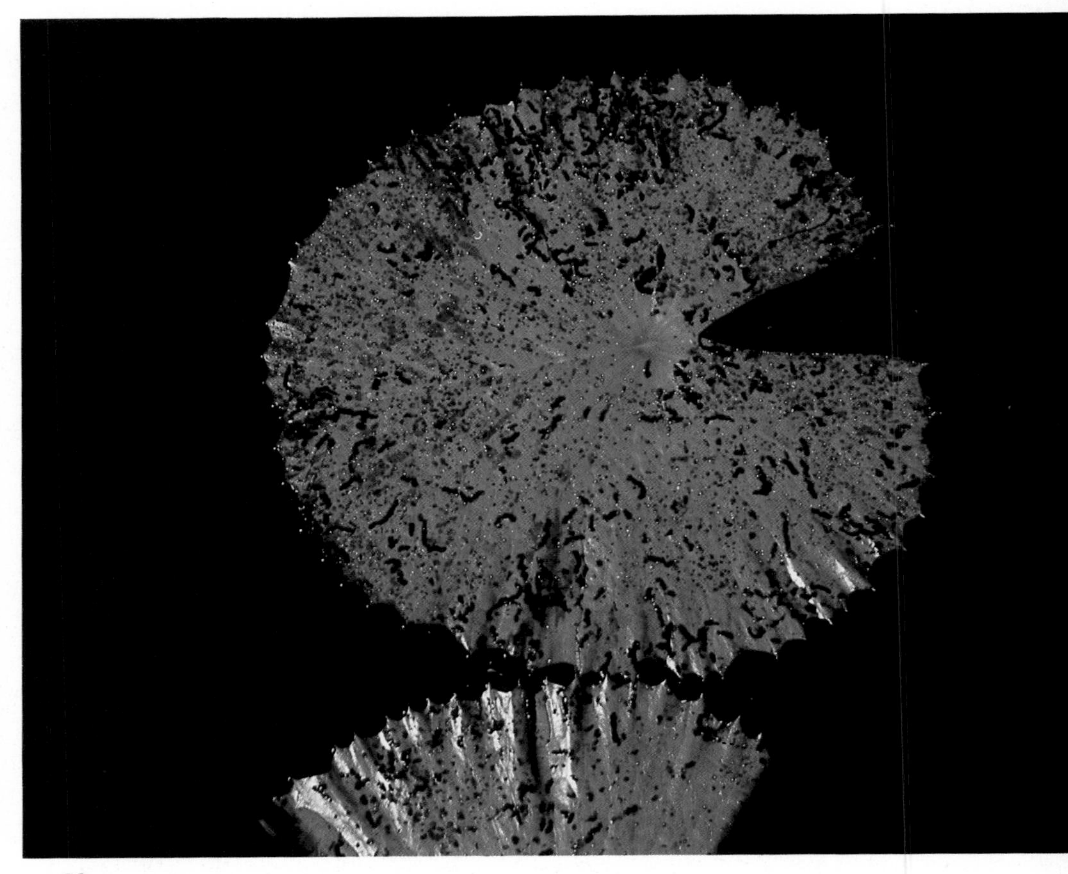

73

74

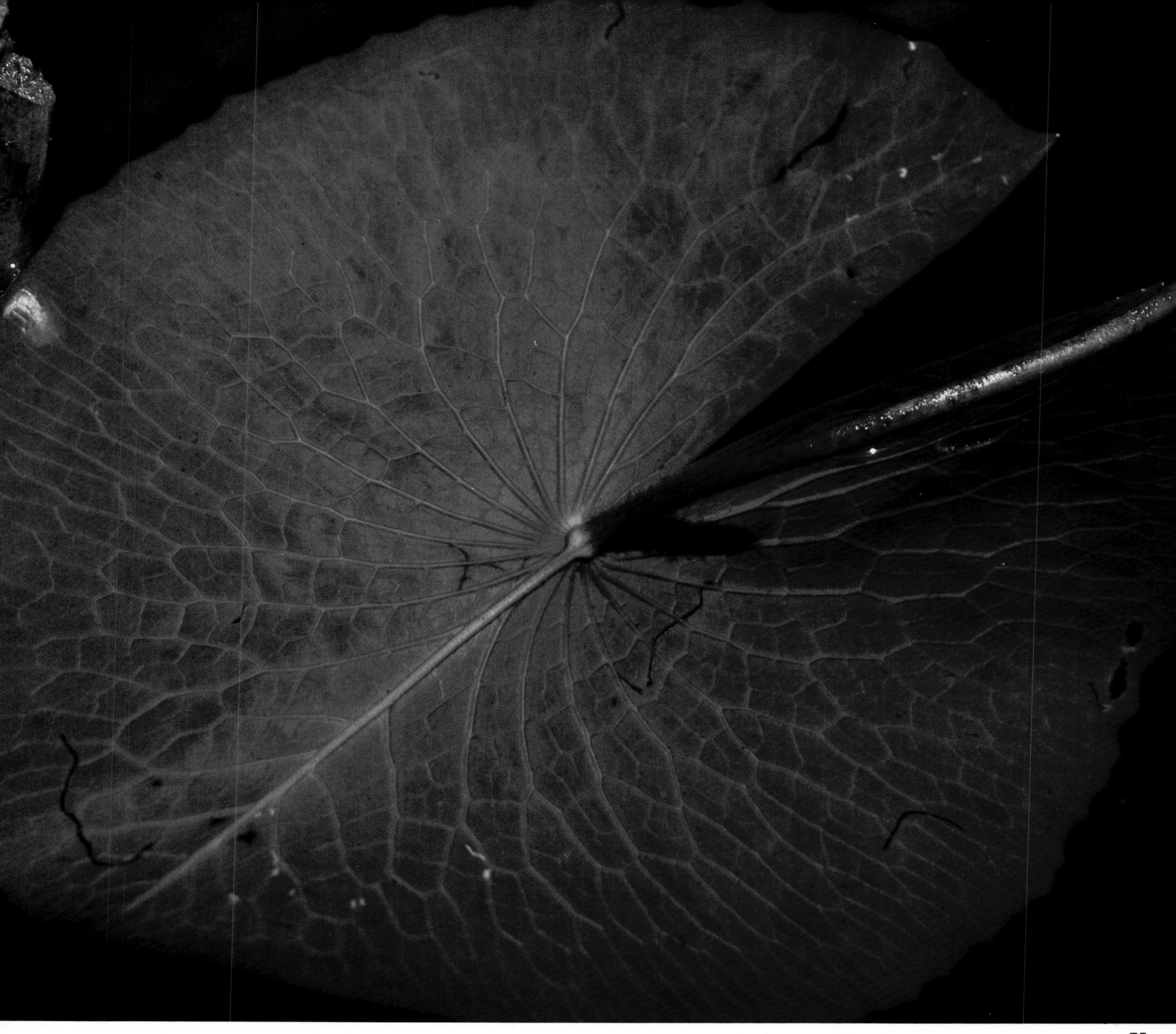

72 Entwined waterlilies slowly open their petals at sunrise. In the evening when darkness falls they will close once more.

73 For this waterlily, as for so many of the Delta's growing things, water forms the link between earth and sky.

74 Not all the wonders of the Okavango Delta are above the water. Here the slow and benevolent flow tugs at an underwater garden.

75 Only fish usually see this view of a wind-tossed lily pad, briefly revealing its claret coloured underside to the world.

76 As a caterpillar this moon moth fed on the leaves of the marula tree, spinning its silvery cocoon on the highest branches.

77 The tell-tale vibrations of a passing fish are picked up by the sensitive legs of a fishing spider, and instantly it dives in pursuit of its dinner.

78 'Don't eat me' warn the conspicuous markings of this fiery grasshopper. Like many insects, it is protected by foul-tasting body juices that no potential aggressor can tolerate. An inexperienced predator might try – but will quickly learn that this meal is a bitter one.

76

77

79 Shimmering spiderwebs in the Okavango Delta. According to a Mbukushu folktale, Nyambi (God) was once but a mere mortal who, irritated by the constant dissatisfaction of his people, went to the spider Diwiwi and asked him to spin him a web to heaven. Once safely there with his wife and son, Nyambi, so the story goes, severed the web cutting himself off forever from the ordinary world.
80 Propelled by pole, paddle or hand, the lowslung mokoro is the ideal vessel from which to see the Okavango.
81 Tall galleries of papyrus enclose the Delta in secrecy. To avoid the lengthy meanderings of the main channels, we sometimes chose a straight course over the waterlogged countryside – a route which only the mokoro can take with ease.

82 A river breeze softly ruffles the crest feathers of a pied kingfisher. This bird is a common sight in the Delta where it demonstrates its skill as a fisherman with a deadly accurate aim. It can hover motionless above the water and once it has made a catch often returns to a favourite perch against which it beats its victim to death before swallowing it.

83 Living up to its name of 'lilytrotter', an African jacana uses its enormous splayed feet to walk on floating vegetation as it searches for insects.

84 Clap, clap, clap, clap . . . a marabou stork announces its arrival at a mixed heronry on Gcodikwe Lagoon. Here wood storks and marabou nest in swamp fig thickets, undisturbed but for occasional visits by egg-eating water monitor lizards.

85 Looking for all the world like weeds and water, a clutch of African jacana eggs rests on floating vegetation, awaiting the return of the mother bird that nonchalantly left the nest, trusting to nature's camouflage as we approached in our mokoro.

86 Like the cast of some vast ice-show spectacular, pond skaters rhythmically glide over the water surface. Feeding on insects that have fallen onto the water, these members of the stinkbug group actually row themselves over the water by means of their long legs.

82

83

84

85

86

87

88

87 Alarmed by wild dog, lechwe splash in elegant arabesques across the Okavango floodplain.

88 Perhaps prettiest of the Okavango's waterfowl, the male pygmy duck whistles softly to its mate in a nearby nest in a hollow tree.

89 A male pygmy duck accompanies his mate back to the nest. These tiny duck feed on the seeds of waterlilies and other swamp plants.

90 Lechwe bound through shallow waters, across an island that began as a termite-mound raised above the flood.

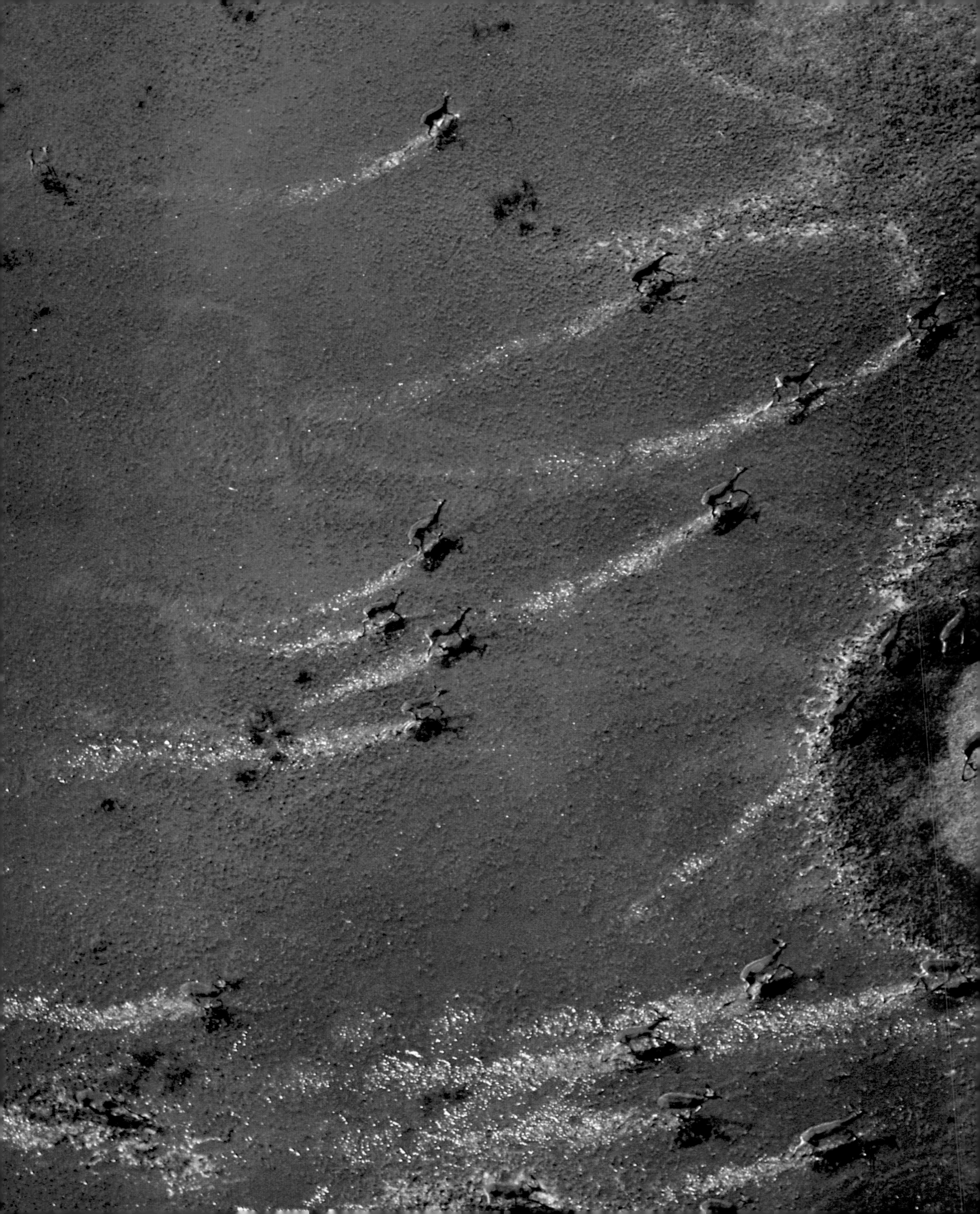

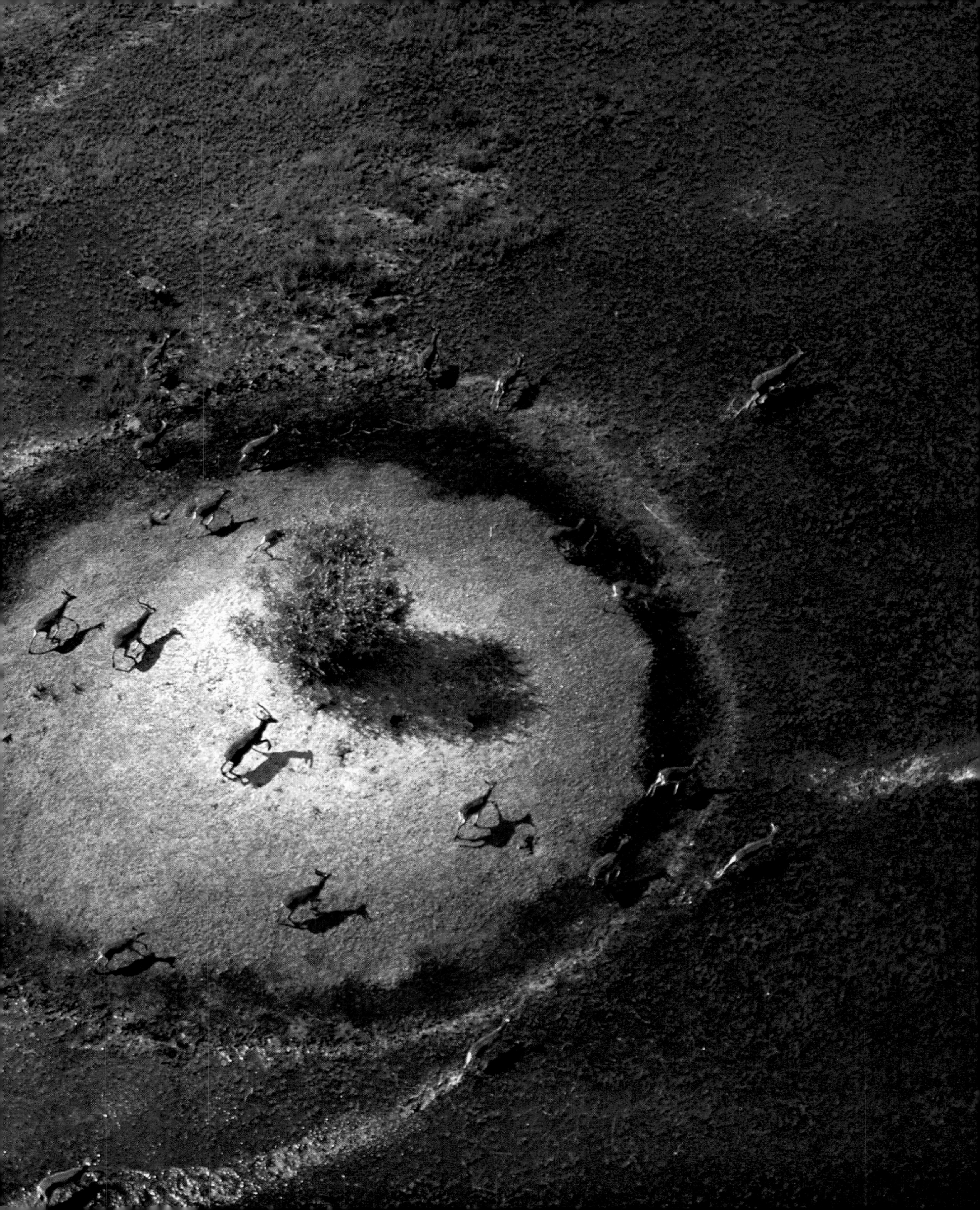

91

91 The little bat-eared fox, this one basking at the entrance of its sandy burrow in an area of open woodland, soon became a familiar sight. Large disc-shaped ears help it detect the sound of insects, lizards and small rodents at night when it feeds.

92 Ripening acacia seeds glow in the first light of morning in Moremi Wildlife Reserve.

93 Playfully pushing and shoving, a pair of young elephant bulls rehearse for the more serious affairs of adulthood, in the dense woodland of the middle Delta.

93

92

94

95

94 Alert to danger, Cape buffalo bulls guard the herd. Often the thunder and splash of hooves is all that reveals the presence of herds within the concealing forest of the Delta islands.

95 Bluffing its way out of trouble, a palm-sized monkey spider puts on a bold aggressive display when cornered. Living underground in a silk-lined burrow, it emerges at night to catch insects.

96 There was a time when the Cape hunting dog was shot on sight. Today the animal is endangered in Africa although packs of them are not uncommon along the Okavango waterfronts.

96

97 As the waters of the high flood recede in the summer months, many isolated pools and small pans remain. At Moremi, zebra drink at a shrinking pond covered with harmless algae.

98 Bathed in the dusky sunlight of a winter morning, impala and guineafowl gather at a pool on the Khwai River in the Moremi Wildlife Reserve.

97

98

99

100

99 Relying on its spots and the dappled light on winter grass for camouflage, a cheetah watches for an unattended foal or weakened animal among a herd of zebra.

100 The zebra, sensing the hidden predator, break into a stampede across the rich grazing grounds of Chief's Island. In the background is a dense stand of mopane woodland.

101

102

101 Just one of the many Okavango islands, unnamed and unknown.

102 Succulent, sweet and fruity, the berries of the motsaodi tree are a favourite with man and monkey alike.

103 Buoyant on their tiny air bladders, *Trapa* plants float freely on the more placid waters of the Delta.

103

104 The termite mound on which this slender mongoose stands to survey his territory gives no hint of the minute architects within that built the two-metre spire. Though there are more than 20 species of termite in the Okavango area, only one of them builds these magnificent and complex structures up to eight metres in height.

105 Beware of thoughtlessly opening the mound, for the jaws of the termite soldiers are something to be reckoned with! The sole task of these heavy-headed individuals is to protect the nest.

106 A soldier keeps guard while workers carry up mud from deep below the nest to repair a hole in the mound.

107 The inner core of the fungus-growing termites' nest is composed of a spongy cork-like material made from the insects' excretions on which they cultivate tiny mushrooms. They feed on these as well as dead grass, dung and wood. Here an immature worker feeds on fungus while a soldier patrols the inner nest for intruders.

108 During the rainy season winged termites leave the nest and fly a few hundred metres before coming to earth and shedding their wings. The females remain still, giving off a scent that attracts the males, who then tap their new-found mates gently with their antennae. As the photograph shows, she then moves off followed by the male to seek a site where they as king and queen can found a new nest.

109 Termite workers constantly lick their queen whose bloated body fills the background of this photograph.

110 After carefully opening the royal cell we photographed the eight centimetre-long queen attended by her many workers. Some were licking her, some feeding her and others removing the thousands of eggs she must lay each day if her children are not to eat her and then replace her with several younger queens from the ranks of the flying termites waiting in the depths of the nest.

111 A termite queen receives regurgitated food from a worker. Although her abdomen has grown enormous, the front part of her body remains the same size as when she founded the nest. The king remains exactly the same size; seemingly overwhelmed he hides out of sight behind his lady.

105

108 109 110

112 113

104

112 After waiting for months if necessary, flying termites begin to emerge in their thousands after the rains on warm summer evenings. Throughout Africa black people relish the flavour of flying termites and use lights to attract the insects when they stream out into the night.

113 A worker carefully removes eggs as they emerge from the queen before placing them in the 'nursery'. Note the tiny springtail insect on the termite's back. Besides these, many other insects have evolved complex relationships with termites and live in mutual association with them in the nest.

114 Within the 'nursery' area of the inner nest an almost mature worker tends eggs and hatchlings, feeding the latter with regurgitated food from its own mouth.

106 107

111

114

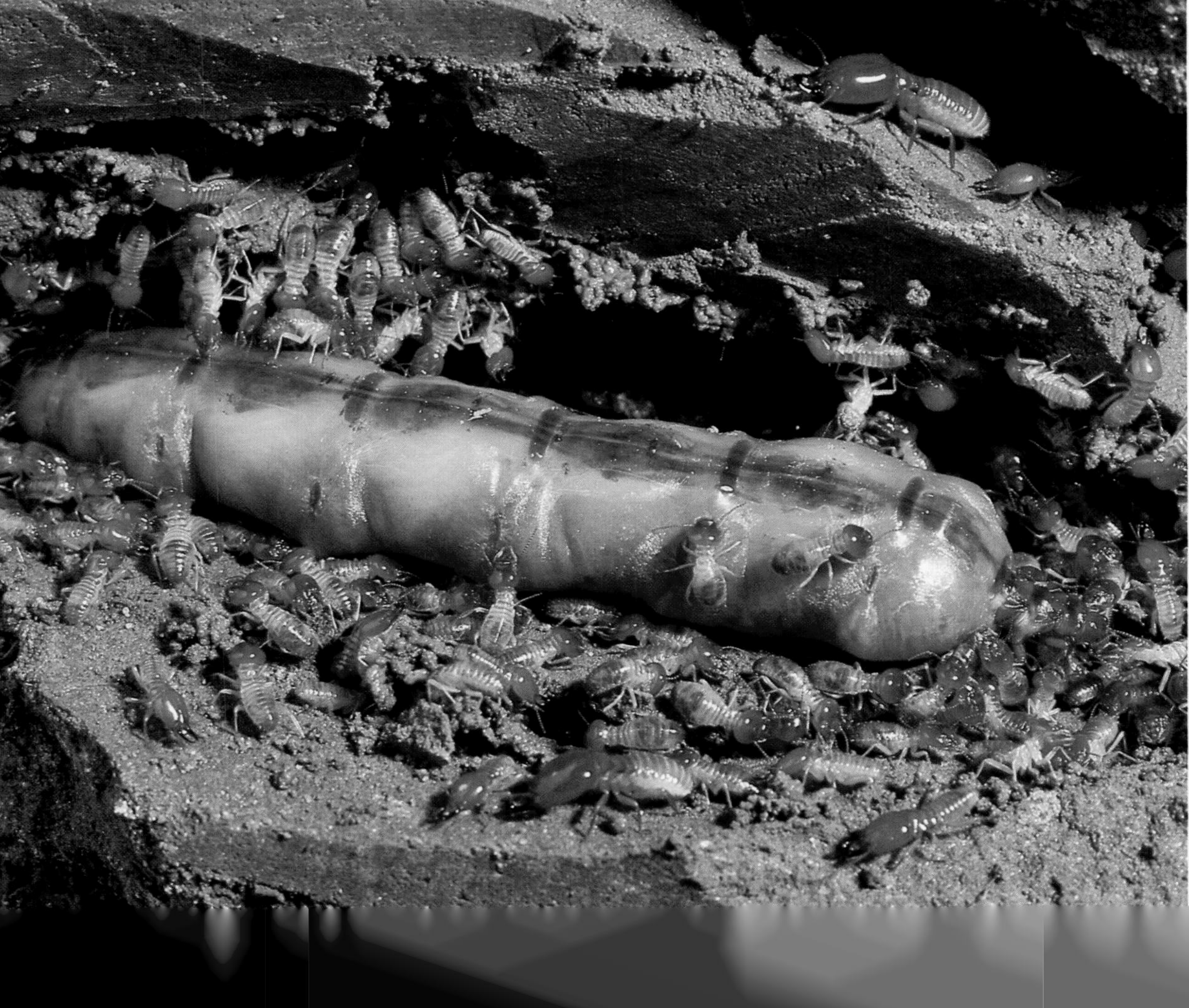

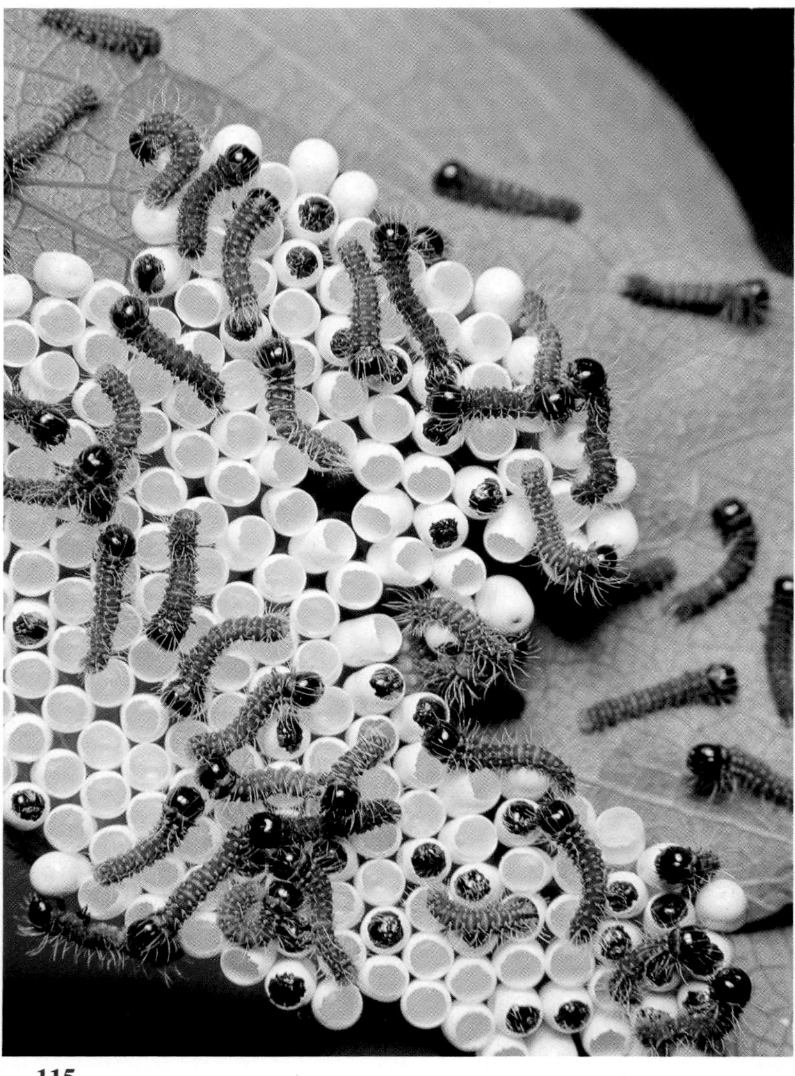

115

115 Tiny caterpillars of the emperor moth wriggle free of eggs laid on the leaves of a mopane tree. No sooner do the caterpillars begin to feed off their leafy nursery than birds swoop down to feed off the caterpillars. Eventually, when they are fully grown, man will eat them too.

116 Time and again as we moved slowly through the Delta we were to see scenes of indescribable beauty. Sometimes we felt ourselves almost bewitched by the colours, the smell of growing things, the changing sky and endless waters – the sheer fecundity of it all.

116

117 Beauty of another sort in a still backwater on the Qugana Lagoon. Decaying vegetation and tiny aquatic ferns create a verdant mat that surrounds a fallen strangler fig.

118 A bird carried the seed and it fell into a crevice in the trunk of a tree where it grew and became this giant strangler fig that entwined its host for over 30 years before finally killing it.

117

118

120

119 A special experience in the Okavango; sunset with hippo grunting as they wake and bellfrogs tuning up for the night's performance.

120 Once night has fallen fruit bats leave their shady daylight retreat in a wild gardenia tree and fly out to seek the wild figs and motsaodi berries on which they feed.

121 Now, as we journeyed south through the Delta we began to come across people once more and we knew that our many weeks of drifting and photographing would soon come to an end. This young boy hid shyly in the foliage as he watched our mokoro pass on the last lap of our long journey that had begun at Shakawe far to the north.

122 Creatures of the sun, dragonflies spend much of their time on activities related to breeding.

123 Fully grown, gaudy and nutritious, these seven centimetre-long mopane worms are harvested wherever the mopane tree grows. The worms are dried and stored by the peoples of the Delta as an all-year-round snack.

119

121

122

123

124

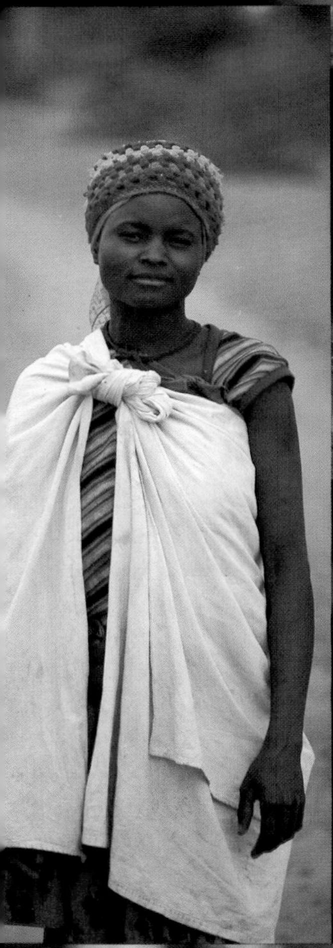

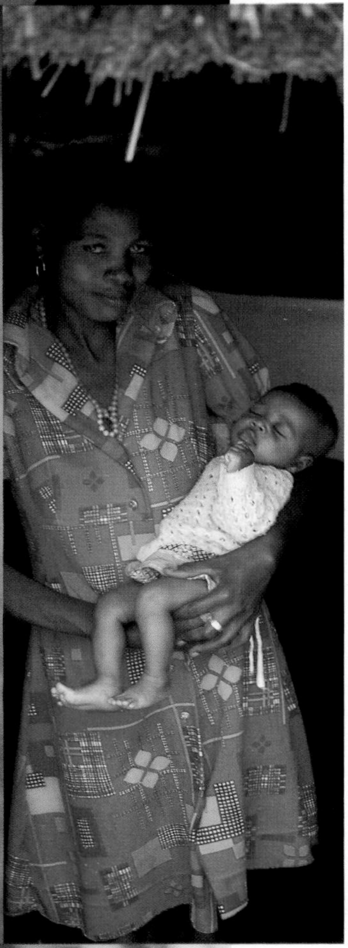

125 126

127

124-127 BaYei, baTawana, ovaHerero . . . on the edge of the swamp they have met and mingled and built their villages together. Man has always lived only on the edge of the Okavango, tied to a narrow 20 kilometre strip that encircles the Delta. Tsetse fly, mosquito and the yearly floods have kept people outside the waterways while drought has confined them equally, pushing them in from the desert.

128 The first part of our journey ends at Maun, for more than 60 years the main village of the Okavango on the southern edge of the swamps. It sprawls across a sandy landscape, trampled bare by man and cattle. Not long ago only a four-wheel drive vehicle could navigate the heavy sand in the middle of the town. Today it boasts a kilometre of tar.

128

The Pans:

Makgadikgadi mirage-blurred enigma etched in salt.

131

130

129 More than 1 000 kilometres away from the sea the Okavango dies among the green salt grasses growing in giant abstract designs over the abandoned lakes of Makgadikgadi.

130 A homestead stirs to a new day along the Boteti River that sustains life for man and beast all the way from just beyond Maun to Makgadikgadi's pans.

131 Before the wheel there was the sled and on the deep sands of this arid country the ox-drawn sledge remains in some respects the more efficient of the two.

132 On the dry wastes of the Kalahari man and his cattle dare never wander far from water. Here, close to the banks of the Boteti River, a stockman herds his cattle to the safety of a kraal for the night.

134

135

133 A remnant of grass, now dried to a golden winter brown, clings to the salty skeleton of Makgadikgadi's lakes.

134 Nata it is called – Nata, the dry river, the river that flows from the north to wither in a parched lake. As we flew overhead, pelican that had stopped to fish the stagnant waters of seasonal pools, scrambled into the air.

135 Orb-web spiders set up a deadly barricade for flying insects beside the Boteti River.

136 A young lion picks over the remains of a giraffe that his pride brought down the previous evening. When he has had his fill he will surrender the carcase to the vultures and hyaena, to the marabou and tiny wagtails, and finally to the maggots and blueflies.

137 Giraffe are a common sight on Nxai Pan where they wander among the tree-covered islands and browse among thorny acacias.

137

138 Dust bursts from the flying hooves of wildebeest as they stampede over one of Makgadikgadi's grassy plains. Wildebeest or gnu are constantly on the move, sometimes covering more than 1 000 kilometres in a single season. Of all the Kalahari's animals they seem the least able to survive that ever-present threat – drought.

139 Imperious predator of Makgadikgadi's skies, the martial eagle hunts on broad wings the boundaries of the plains. Using thermals to gain height, it searches for ostrich chicks and korhaan.

140

140 The Bushmen believe that it was the ostrich that first brought fire to the world, but the bird jealously kept it tucked under its wing lest anyone should steal it. By a trick man managed to obtain the secret, but to this day the ostrich refuses to use its wings to fly for fear that any other creature might steal its secret too.

141 Game trails thread the plains and like the thousands of wild animals that have gone before, a herd of zebra makes its way towards the life-giving brown waters of the Boteti River.

142 Here today, gone tomorrow. Thousands of greater flamingo grace the ephemeral but nutrient-rich waters of Makgadikgadi. After rains the arid wastes can be transformed seemingly overnight into immense shallow pans of blue water.

141

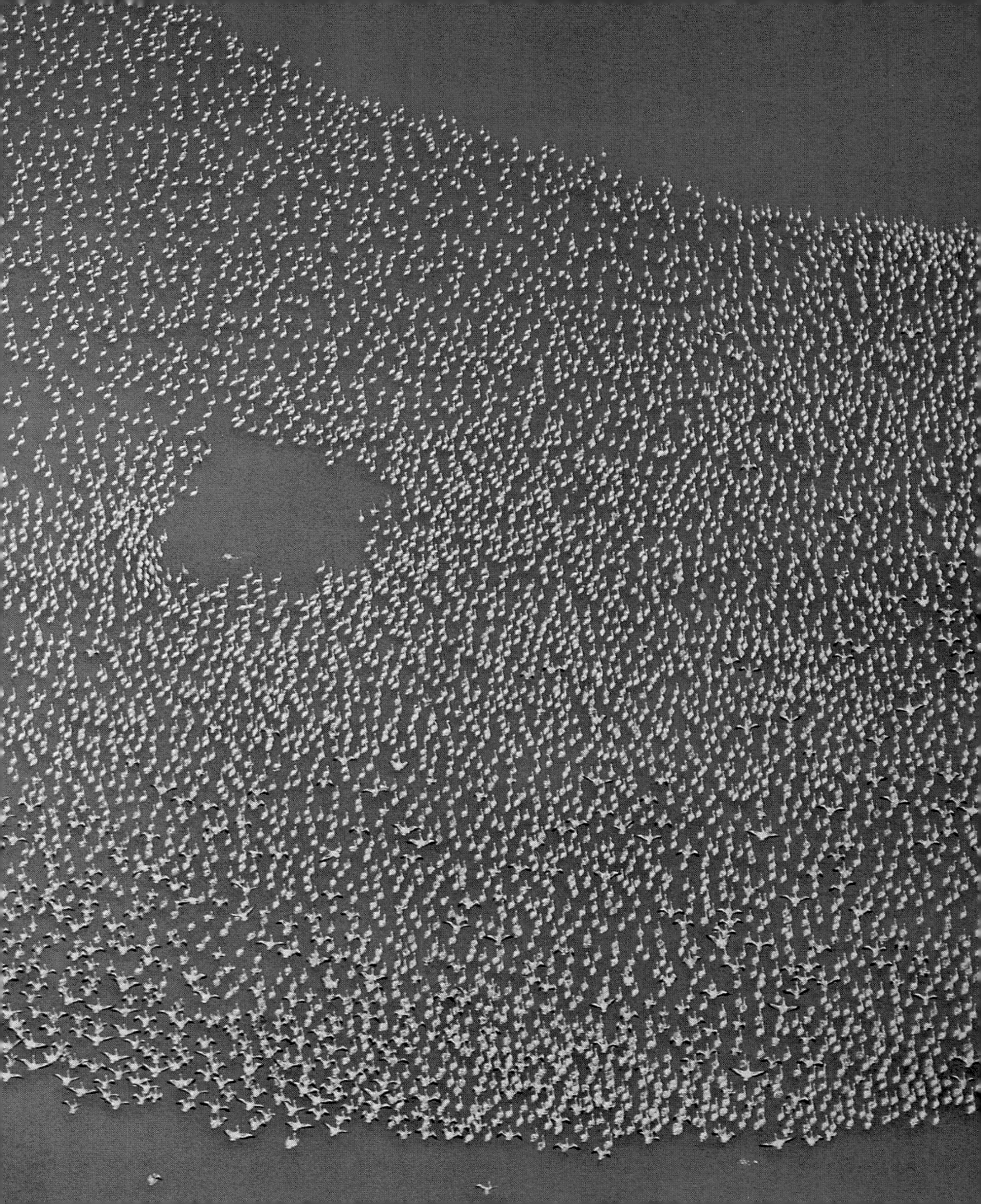

143 A lone pelican feather, symbol of the splendour of Makgadikgadi's great gathering of birds in the rainy season, now half a year past.

144 While heavy rains may briefly flood Makgadikgadi, the shallow lakes soon evaporate leaving only salt crystals to glitter under the desert sky.

The Game Reserves:

From water, sky and boundless plains life springs in wild profusion.

146

145 Here's spit in your eye! An elephant squirts an aggressive spray of water as we intrude on his territory.

146 From its perch above the plain a brown snake eagle keeps a look-out for reptilian coils that promise its next meal.

147

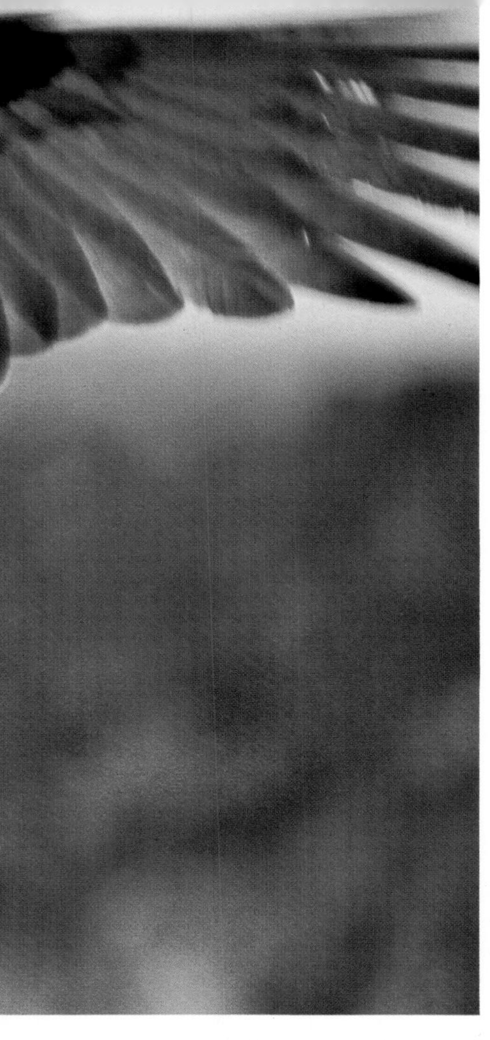

147 Animals are drawn to the edge of the rising flood. Attentive but unafraid, these waterbuck lift their heads from the floodplain of the Chobe River.

148 A water monitor, that may grow to more than two metres in length, surveys its riverside kingdom. Alert eyes and nostrils detect frogs, chicks and eggs that form this reptile's diet. Only moments later this great lizard lashed out at us with its heavy tail and fled back into the water.

149 Three egrets search the shallows of the Linyanti Marsh for fish, tadpoles and insects.

150 Africa's most deadly snake, the black mamba, every year accounts for several lives. Although not deliberately aggressive, it is quick to defend itself if it feels threatened.

150

148

149

151 For a hundred years great trees grew in the white sands of the dry Savuti channel. Then, suddenly and inexplicably the river began to flow again in 1957; now the drowned trunks cast their gallows-stark reflections on the water.

152 A wattled crane elegantly probes the margins of the Savuti Marsh for lily bulbs and sleeping frogs.

151

152

153 The Linyanti is a two-way river – one year its waters will flow this way, another year it will reverse its flow. But the vagaries of the current are of little concern to the hippo that peer with periscope eyes at visitors to the cool channels.
154 Aw shucks, am I really so beautiful?

155

155 An autumn fire moving across the nearby Savuti Marsh casts a muted filter over the sun at Gubatsha Hills. These huge conflagrations create their own turbulent air currents and at Savuti the smoke is sometimes so dense that the sun appears to set mid-afternoon. Small aeroplanes are turned away, unable to land in the pall.

156 With expectant bill and purposeful step a wood ibis searches a Linyanti waterway for insects, molluscs, fish and frogs.

157 The jigsaw pattern of scorched earth in the foreground is record of the many months that the countryside surrounding the Savuti Channel is without rain. Then each year in late winter the Savuti (in the background) gradually floods over the plains of the Mababe Depression to transform the parched landscape into lush marsh and grassland.

156

158, 159, 160 'This part of the country must have been utterly undisturbed by human beings', remarked the famous hunter and naturalist Frederick Selous when he gazed at Chobe's abundant herds 100 years ago. The ground still shakes to the thunder of hooves as thousands of animals follow the scent of grass and water. Here zebra (158), impala (159) and Cape buffalo (160) move across the plains of Savuti.

161

161 Elephant, buffalo, zebra – animals as far as the eye can see in the Savuti marshlands.

162 Big animals bring big problems. Each elephant in this marching procession needs 250 kilograms of greenery a day, and Chobe's woodland has suffered in recent years as elephant from many areas take sanctuary in the park.

163

164

163 From a lofty eyrie in a knob-thorn a fish eagle pauses before feeding its six-week-old chick.

164 Over much of Africa the sable antelope is endangered for it is sensitive to change in its grazing and has retreated as the grasslands alter under man's influence. On the Chobe riverside a herd of this beautiful antelope make a forest of horns as they sniff upwind.

165 For more than a century Chobe has been one of Africa's great hunting grounds. While some parts of this northern wilderness are reserved for tribal and professional hunting, huge expanses have been set aside as national parkland where herds of sable, wildebeest and many other animals share the woodland.

166

167

168

166 A heap of bones and scraggy skin – all that is left from the lions' kill, but it makes a meal for the spotted hyaena. Vultures waiting in the nearby tree will soon flap down to the carcase to peck at the remnants – and the bone fragments that are essential to their diet. Some of the bone chips will be carried back to the vultures' nestlings that depend on this source of calcium if they are to be viable in adulthood.

167 Performing a vital role in keeping the veld free of decaying flesh, vultures rip and tear at the last shreds of a buffalo carcase. These heavy birds use thermals to soar high into the sky in search of carrion. As soon as one dips and descends to a kill it is immediately spotted by the keen eyes of others of its kind which glide down to demand their share.

168 While scavengers jostle and squabble over the leftovers of the kill, a sleek lion and his mate turn their attention to amorous matters.

169

169 Gemsbok graze the dry grasses of a scorched plain. The oryx, or gemsbok, well deserves its reputation as a formidable adversary quick to use its rapier-like horns. By virtue of a special adaptation in its nose which helps cool blood reaching its brain, this antelope is able to survive the high temperatures of the desert.

170 A lioness lies sleepily curled in the sedges of the treeless Savuti Marsh.

171 Termite mounds offer the only elevation above the flatness of Savuti. Here a lioness keeps look-out for a possible meal for the pride.

170

172

173

172 Elephant dust the dawn as they make their way across Chobe's broad marshes.

173 The short, the fat and the tall at a dwindling pool. Elephant share the last of the water with a lone hippopotamus and a gangling giraffe.

174 *Lehututu,* expressive local name for the ground hornbill. Turkey-sized and aggressive, this bird makes its distinctive call to keep in contact with members of its family group as it swaggers about looking for food.

174

175

176

177

175 A lone white rhino dwarfed by the sheer scale of its feeding grounds in the Mababe Depression. 'The number of rhinoceroses destroyed annually in South Africa is very considerable', reported explorer hunter Charles John Andersson when he hunted in Botswana more than 100 years ago. He went on: 'Messrs Oswell and Vardon killed, in one year, no less than 89 of these animals; on my present journey I myself shot single-handed nearly two thirds of this amount.' By the turn of the century the white rhino had disappeared from the Chobe area and only recently was the animal re-introduced.

176 Carmine bee-eaters – one of Africa's most beautiful birds – hover above the Linyanti airstrip where thousands of them lay their eggs in shallow sand burrows away from the river, their flashing red wings a real hazard to the aircraft that make infrequent landings on the birds' terrain. The Linyanti breeding ground is the only known flat-land colony of this species.

177 Just some of the thousands of carmine bee-eaters that nest in burrows along the Chobe River, their endless comings and goings transforming parts of the riverbank into a spectacle of glorious colour. The colonies of these birds are world-famous.

178 The white rhino, no paler than the thorntree-browsing black rhino. 'White' is probably a corruption of 'wide', referring to its rough broad lips with which it tears out grass.

178

179 Snorkelling its way across the Linyanti River an elephant makes for the succulent papyrus beds on the opposite bank.

180 With no more than an occasional twitch, an elephant trapped in a mud wallow lives out its last moments.

181 Through a leafy canopy, two bull elephant strip branches of foliage and bark to feed. In this way the excessive elephant population has modified much of Chobe's riverside area, turning patches of open woodland into dense bush.

179

180

182 A skyline of giraffe at Savuti.

183

183 Caught in the light of our spotlight, a fish eagle stares implacably at the camera.

184 Cape hunting dogs are the wolves of Africa. At a rainwater pan they share a drink with double-banded sandgrouse before loping off into the night.

185 Thousands of roosting red-billed quelea can break tree branches with their weight. Widely acknowledged as the 'avian locust', these birds have been known to roost literally feather to feather over tens of hectares of scrubland.

184

Lake Ngami:

Ngami half-remembered legend half-forgotten lake.

186 A Herero woman, her dress a proud symbol of group identity, relaxes outside her hut on the shores of Lake Ngami. Herero women stubbornly refuse to abandon the style of dress they inherited from German missionaries in the 19th century.

187 Lake Ngami: sometimes a dusty depression, sometimes a 200 square kilometre lake.

188 Nowhere else has man hugged the Okavango so close for so long. This is Ngami today – a lake where marabou storks pace the shallows, where cattle wade chest-deep to feed in the water, while further from the featureless shoreline fishermen set their nets.

187

189 Seventy years ago the ovaHerero came fleeing across the Kalahari Desert, fugitives from a war of extermination in Namibia. Many of them died on the sand before the survivors reached the Okavango, people without a possession in the world. They offered their new country all that was left to them – their labour – and became a race of servants. Slowly they reversed their apparent fate, building up afresh the herds which they had had to leave behind, until today they are among the biggest cattle-owners – and therefore among the wealthiest people – of the Delta.

190 Across the emptiness of the plain the visitor is sighted already a long way away, and hot sweet tea is waiting for the traveller, weary from the desert.

191 These three young flamingos will eventually come to know many of Africa's great lakes and pans during their lives of migration.

189

191

190

193

192 A good catch for today. When the lake has water it supports a small fishing village on its shores and then its dried bream are sold as far afield as Rhodesia and Namibia.

193 Half a continent away from their seashore home, grey-headed gulls join sacred ibis and marabou storks at Ngami's offal pits where, in good years, the fishing company dumps its wastes.

194 Though dung-beetles work overtime, the surroundings of Ngami still offer the flies ample cow-pats in which to breed. With so many flies everywhere it is little wonder that this young herdboy simply ignores them.

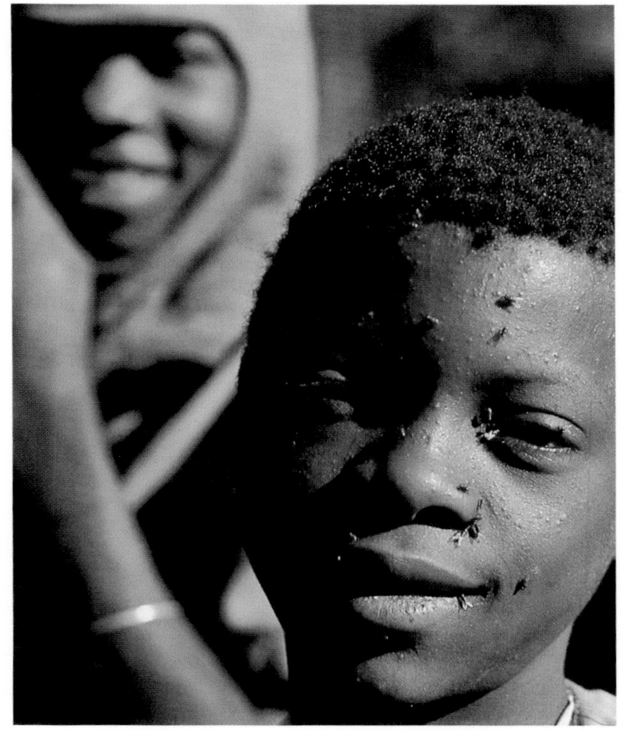

194

195

197

195 Glinty-eyed at being disturbed, this 18 centimetre-long bullfrog might well look annoyed. Moments earlier his wintertime burrow had been uncovered by a cow's hoof. With the first heavy rains of summer these giant amphibians emerge from hibernation by the hundreds
to consume toads, lizards, chicks and rodents.

196

196 While water is an unpredictable commodity at Ngami, dust is a constant. Wherever there is water and there are cattle in Botswana, a dustbowl is born. One survey of boreholes showed that within 11 years of a borehole having been drilled, a denuded zone 12 kilometres-wide had grown around the watering-point. And since Ngami is one of the Kalahari's largest watering places, it is also one of its most punished.

197 Miniature demons in the dust, ant-lions wait hidden at the bottoms of the tiny conical pits they have dug in the hope that a passing ant will stumble in. Pencil-fine tracks show their random wanderings.

198 Not as dangerous as it looks, this half-metre long sand snake is harmless to man and feeds on lizards.

199

199 Storks roost in the dead trees around Lake Ngami. The trees grew when the lake was empty and then drowned when a flood returned 50 years later to fill it once more. But these Abdim storks do not nest here; they will fly hundreds of kilometres north to breed when winter comes to Botswana.

200 Marabou storks stand hunched in Ngami's shallows. The lake of today gives no hint of its former glory. Gone are the wild herds and papyrus, replaced by man and his livestock. Yet in those years that Ngami contains water, it takes on a new magic as thousands upon thousands of waterfowl converge to feast upon it.

201 Marabou storks at Lake Ngami.

202 White pelican punch the water with their big webbed feet as they take to the air above the legendary lake – Lake Ngami.

200

201